CHRISTMAS WITH KATE

*A Treasury of Christmas Stories
from the Pages of Heart of the Home*

Editor
Samantha Adams

Assistant to the Editor
Patricia Patterson Thompson

Production and Illustrations
Bruce Bealmear

Copyright © 1994
by Capper Press
Printed in the United States of America

ISBN: 0-941678-45-8

Dear Readers:

Year after year, Capper's readers have taken us into their homes to share the joy and humor of their most touching Christmas moments.

As you read this book, you will revisit old friends who will share their holiday traditions, make you laugh about Christmas pageants that took unexpected turns, give you a glimpse at long-ago Christmases, and share unique ideas about the beautiful decorations they use and the cherished traditions they celebrate in their homes during the holidays.

When I was a child, Christmas was a magical time. The Christmas tree was the heart of our celebration. Dad loved to take the family out several days before Christmas to select a tree—and he liked a big one. As a family, we had our own idea of just how a perfect tree should be shaped; how tall it should be and how fat. There were prolonged discussions and viewings of countless trees as we stamped our feet in the frigid snow, burrowing deeper into our mufflers until just the right one was found. Then came the fun of decorating the tree together until it took on all the magical wonder of the holiday season.

Our tree decorations were plain by today's standards, but we thought they were beautiful. When we were young and money was scarce, Mother covered a small cardboard star with shiny silver foil to put atop the tree. Even later, when we could afford a "fancy" treetop ornament, a foil-covered cardboard star always meant Christmas to me. I still use one on my tree today.

Christmas Eve meant carols and a hushed candlelight service at the church, where the true meaning of Christmas was rediscovered.

Then at last, Christmas morning would arrive. We would awaken early and bound downstairs in pajamas to see what Santa Claus had left. With its flurry of presents, stockings bulging with nuts, fruit and hard candies; the heavenly aromas of turkey, stuffing, pies and cakes mingling; the excited chatter and laughter of cousins and aunts and uncles arriving to share a bountiful dinner, Christmas was indeed a festive occasion. The cold and snowy landscape outside our frosted windowpanes made the day complete.

I hope the stories in this book remind you of your very best Christmases and the special people in your life who shared them with you.

May a warm and wonderful old-fashioned Christmas be yours. And the best of wishes for the year ahead!

Love,
Kate Marchbanks

CONTENTS

Cherished Sentiments

Chapter 1

O F ALL THE things we give and receive at Christmas time, a simple greeting card is often the most appreciated. The tradition dates back to Victorian England and was popularized in America by lithographer Louis Prang during the 1870s.

Today, Christmas cards come in every size, shape and color. Some of my readers say that they prefer those that are in tune with the traditional meaning of Christmas, while others appreciate any card with a personal message inside.

Whatever their pleasure, few people would disagree that these annual greetings have become an integral part of their holiday celebration.

Linger Over Your Cards

Don't rush down that list, madly addressing Christmas cards—any way to get the job done. Take time to remember and enjoy your memories.

Those names represent your life history—its joys, sorrows and friendships. One is an old family friend you haven't seen for years, another a favorite old-time teacher, the family doctor, your relatives, a sick child who must spend Christmas away from home. With regret mark off that friend who died since last year's cheery card reached him.

Once a year is seldom enough to really think about

OLD FRIENDS. December 10, 1949

Would Sure Miss Greeting Cards

It would be very hard to decide on only one Christmas ritual. I love them all, but I can't imagine the Christmas season without an evergreen tree or greeting cards.

Exchanging cards is the only way I keep in touch with many relatives and friends. A short note or a few scribbled words, once a year, keeps me informed of any important events or changes in their lives.

As the cards come in, I display them around the fireplace mantel on a red ribbon swag. They are decorative and colorful, as well as a topic of conversation.

Then there is the tree. I like searching out the right one from among the hundreds available. I prefer the small bushy size, which will fit in almost any place.

As much as I look forward to the tree trimming, I believe Christmas cards would be my first choice. A fireplace mantel, large plants or tables, etc., can always be decorated in place of a tree. Nothing can take the place of a Christmas card wishing you a happy

HOLIDAY. December 13, 1977

Recycling The Cards

Save the Christmas cards you receive. I use these cards to make cards for the next year. Using the fronts, with the picture, I cut off any rough edges to make it neat all around. With a red or green pen I write a poem or message and the address on the back. Stick a Christmas seal here and there, add a postage stamp and mail THEM. January 11, 1977

Cards Make A Nice Gift

I have been a shut-in for a year and a half. Last Christmas my most thoughtful gift was a package of personally selected cards. Birthday, convalescent, sympathy, thinking of you, etc., were included. My dear daughter-in-law included stamps, but the cards alone would make a nice gift for anyone unable to shop.

Many do not think of cards as a gift. They can be bought any time you are shopping, even weeks in advance. Don't forget to include some humorous ONES. December 26, 1978

Writes To Former Army Sisters

Twenty-nine Christmases ago, I corresponded with 100 WACs. Previous to this, I served in the Army three years. Corresponding with 100 WACs posed a problem. I made it less a chore by mimeographing my letters, but only at Christmas time.

Now, 29 years later, my list has dwindled to 25. Many have changed addresses, failing to notify me. Others, busy with families and full lives, can't find the time. Some passed away. Most of the 25 will write letters; others pen notes on cards. Four have individual ways of presenting their yearly letters.

Mabel, who teaches school in California and has two teen-age girls, sends a mimeographed travelogue of her summer activities. Every summer, she and her girls take a scenic trip here in the States.

Eleanor, an artist, paints her message on her own designed

3

cards. Designs show what's happening now with a cheery Yuletide flavor.

Another friend goes in for amateur photography. She, her husband, children and grandchildren are posed in a sequence of yearly events in one composite picture.

Eloise gives me the biggest bang in her newspaper-type letters. Her husband manages a weekly. Her letter are printed like a miniature newspaper. Examples of headlines are: "Ghost Town Target for Next Summer's Vacation," "Got the Pioneer Spirit? Cut Your Own Christmas Tree Here," "Swimming? Take Your Choice, Hot Springs or Cold Streams," "River Rats Find Aquatic Thrills in Floating Down River." You get the picture. It's what's going on in her life and town.

Annual Christmas letters from former Army sisters, relatives and friends enhance Christmas happiness for my husband and me on our

FARM. December 3-10, 1974

"Thought" Notes

If one is unable to buy Christmas cards this year, an excellent substitute is to write a good letter, or note, to friends one has neglected during the year. A Christmas seal stuck on the writing paper gives the Christmas touch.

MRS. ALVIN FALCH. December 19, 1931

Delivers Card

After my husband retired from a large insurance company, he wanted to keep in touch with another retiree by means of a Christmas card each year. The only problem was he had lost his friend's address.

It looked hopeless until he decided to take a chance by putting his friend's description instead of his address on the card. He gave his name, former position in the insurance company, his personal appearance: "Short, fat, jovial." As an extra clue he added, "Hobbies:

channel cat fishing and weekend golf." Then he ended with the town and state.

Much to my husband's delight, a few days before Christmas, he received an answer. It was filled with laughter and praise for my husband's ingenuity, and the post office's resourcefulness in locating him with such meager information.

I think too often we tend to criticize our postal service and overlook the services it performs that aren't in the regular line of
DUTY. December 18-25, 1973

Daughter's Taste Better Than Mother's

One recent Christmas, my daughter and her husband came from Denver for a visit. After Christmas, we went shopping in the city for Christmas bargains. My daughter found some Christmas cards that were $10 a box marked down to $1. She told me to buy some, but I didn't like the picture on them.

She assured me they were "beautiful," so I bought a box. On the way home, she told her husband of the great bargain "Mom" got on the Christmas cards. He asked: "Did you get some too?" She replied: "No, I didn't like them."

Right then and there I decided she would receive every one of those cards next Christmas!

Several weeks before the next Christmas, I distributed this box of cards to friends and relatives far and wide and explained why they should send this card to my daughter. As Christmas drew closer, she commented to me on how many cards she was getting from all over the country that were exactly alike. She could not understand why so many selected that card, as they weren't all that great.

She would hold up the card and say to her husband, who was in on the joke: "Look, just what is so special about this card that so many people bought it?"

She finally made the connection, and got as good a laugh out of it as did everyone who sent her the
CARDS. December 21, 1993

Use For Christmas Cards

Christmas cards of parchment as well as many other kinds work up well into colorful lampshades.

Save your Christmas cards to put in the foreign missionary box. Send them to little children in the hospitals in far-away lands, where there'll be no end to their enjoyment.

AMY HUNT. December 24, 1932

"Canned" Sentiments

I have a friend who is furious every time she receives a greeting card that contains nothing but a printed sentiment and a hastily scrawled signature.

I think I agree with her, for after all, why should we spend several cents for a card, an additional 3 cents for a stamp and then not even bother to include a note of our personal interests? The only contact many folks have is through annual greeting cards, and one might at least take the time to outline the year's activities, future hopes and present state of health.

I.H.N. December 15, 1934

Stamps And Cards

This year, if you can possibly afford it, let the envelope that contains your Christmas greeting cards to best beloved ones also contain war stamps or bonds. You'll get personal pleasure from having invested in victory; and, your gift recipient will derive "purse"nal satisfaction from the "present" with a "future."

MEXIKANSAN. December 19, 1942

Christmas Cards

The other day I came across my last Christmas cards.

One of them pictured a cover with a kitten landing in a parachute, wishing me a Merry Christmas.

Another was of a dog, pushing a baby buggy of scrambling

puppies. She, too, hoped I'd have a nice holiday.

I'd like to boycott all those kind of cards, and wish my friends would, too.

A card with a sketch of a long-eared puppy howling out "Best Wishes" to me has nothing distinctive of Christmas about it.

Our Savior was born on Christmas Day. We are happy about it and should at least give him this day.

Let us send cards commemorating the joy of Christ's birth, and our friends will know our thought is true and sincere.

A MOTHER. December 14, 1946

Buckshot Never Received His Card

It was Christmas 1949. I was 6 years old and in love. The little boy was named Loren, but everybody called him Buckshot. His clothes were so ragged and full of holes they looked as though they'd been blasted with a shotgun.

Loren was so poor. He was skin and bones and didn't even own a winter coat. When I looked at him, I saw his beautiful eyes and the sweetest smile in the world.

I bought the prettiest Christmas card I could find and signed it, "I love you. From your Secret Girlfriend."

I sat next to him at the class party, and my heart pounded so loudly I was sure all the kids could hear it. I kept waiting for the right time to give him the card, but it never came.

I was afraid the kids would tease me about being in love with the poorest boy in town. Or, what if he laughed and showed my card to everyone. I didn't give him the card. I took it home and hid it in my secret treasure box. We moved away and I never saw Loren again.

I kept the card 41 years and must have looked at it a thousand times. I still get tears in my eyes when I think of that special little boy. I wonder what would have happened if I'd given him the Christmas card that said, "I love you."

I'm 47 years old now and have never

MARRIED. December 18, 1990

7

Musical Christmas Card Conveys Mom's Message

Last Christmas, my dear wife, Edith, was seriously ill. One of the greetings we received was a folder that played "Silent Night" when opened. All Christmas cards received were placed in an open cardboard container. After the holidays, they were relegated to a shelf in the laundry room.

In late February, my dear wife of 48 years passed away. The day after the funeral, daughter Vera was busy in the laundry room when the musical Christmas card opened up just far enough to begin "Silent Night." This occurred several times until Vera put the card flat on the shelf and weighted it down with a small, white flower-bud vase.

That night our daughters, Carol and Gail, who lived some distance away, stayed overnight and occupied a bedroom directly across the hall from the laundry room.

In the morning, they woke early and lay there talking. One said, "Before we go home today, I wish we could have some sign from Mom, so we would know she is all right."

Not long afterward, they heard music, a Christmas song. They heard it again and alerted me. I thought it might be one of our phones off the hook or the smoke detector, but that wasn't it.

Later, when daughters Rita and Vera arrived, the four girls discussed the mysterious music. Then one of the girls asked about the Christmas card. Vera went into the laundry to search for it. She removed the white vase and the card opened slightly. "Sleep in heavenly peace" was heard.

Carol and Gail raced to the laundry room from another part of the house. "Where is it coming from? That's the sound. That's what we've been hearing."

How could this have happened? The card had been lying flat with a flower vase on top to keep it closed. It would not play the music unless the folder was opened. There could be only one explanation: an unexplained force had raised that vase! Here's something else: we heard the music four times, and my dear wife and I reared four daughters.

Carol and Gail had hoped for a sign from Mom that she was all

right. I'm convinced they got it. The message—"sleep in heavenly peace"—is certainly plain. Mom is in heavenly
PEACE. December 22, 1987

Shows Her Cards

About two weeks before Christmas I put a white tablecloth on the table, then cover it with a clear plastic cloth. When Christmas cards begin to arrive I put them under the plastic. This makes a pretty table and is a good way to display your
CARDS. December 4-11, 1962

CHRISTMAS WITH KATE

The Seasonal Spotlight

Chapter 2

*E*VERY YEAR, CHRISTMAS pageants and programs put on by the local school or church give children a chance to perform their favorite carols and parents an opportunity to see their little angels in the spotlight. The performance seldom goes exactly as planned, but nobody seems to mind. In fact, the biggest blunder of the show usually gets the most applause!

My readers have sat through a few Christmas programs, and their recollections are both funny and touching. As you read these, don't be surprised if you catch yourself remembering when you or your children stood in the seasonal spotlight.

Santa Was Still In The Audience

My poem was the last thing in the Christmas program. My mother had written it, mentioning nearly everyone in the one-room school by name. The last line was, "I think I hear sleigh bells, it must be Santa." Santa was to enter at that point.

Somehow I found out the teacher had asked Dad to play Santa that year. I felt really grown-up to be in on the secret. I was in several plays and songs. Every time I was on stage, there was Dad, big as life, enjoying the program. It came time for my poem and sure enough, there was Dad, still in the audience. I sure dreaded that closing line because I was convinced Santa wasn't going to come through the door; but say it I must. Thru the door came the jolly old gent himself, sleigh bells and all!

When Santa called my name and handed me a gift, I looked into his eyes and recognized
GRANDPA. December 8, 1981

Elves Make Rapid Scenery Changes

My first-grade class was presenting a Christmas pageant, and we adults solved the problems of having two background settings. We had the upper-grade children paint a forest scene on one side of a huge piece of cardboard and a workshop scene on the other. The play was about the elves taking gifts to forest animals after working for Santa in his shop.

All those 6-year-olds got enthusiastic when they understood the play. I stood in the corner to signal when the elves were to reverse the cardboard from workshop scene to forest scene. When I gave the signal, they whirled the cardboard around like a hurricane. The audience started laughing and continued laughing throughout the play. Those parents didn't listen to the script. They just whooped and hollered when the tiny elves in red suits grabbed the scenery. The more the audience laughed, the faster the elves turned the scenery.

The play was deemed a success by parents of the
ELVES. December 8, 1987

Sister Couldn't Resist

Looking angelic in her angel costume, 3-year-old Tonya stood by the side of the manger scene in the Christmas program. Her big brother was a shepherd. When he came in and knelt down at the side of the manger, head touching the floor, Tonya, quick as a wink jumped astride her brother yelling, "Get up horsie."

This brought down the house! Her brother was dying of
EMBARRASSMENT! December 22, 1987

Little Shepherd Takes Role Seriously

Several years ago when I was fairly new at my church, I happened to be helping with the nativity scene. It was hard work coordinating parts for the right children. They were excited and worked hard to learn verses and songs.

There was one small 4-year-old boy who was to be a shepherd. Someone told him a story about how important the shepherd was in protecting the sheep from wolves. He was elated to be a shepherd boy.

There were not enough canes for each shepherd to have a staff, but seeing how eager the boy was, we went the extra mile to find a staff for him.

As the shepherds came on stage, the imagination of this youngster took over. He raised his cane to his shoulder, aimed at the audience and with audible sound effects, began to shoot the "wolves."

His older brother, who was a short distance away in the choir, tried in vain to get the child's attention. Finally the shepherd turned around and shot his brother, evidently just one more bothersome wolf.

About this time the reading had ended and the piano began to play. The children began to sing, thus ending the imaginary role-playing of the young shepherd.

I've laughed many times about that
SCENE. December 8, 1987

13

Children Present Moving Christmas Play At Church

One night in December 1941, the White Heath School gave a Christmas program. There was no stage in the schoolhouse, so the teachers asked permission to use the stage in the church. I was a member of the church and was there to hear my Sunday School class perform their recitations and songs.

When it was time for the upper grades to present the play, the lights dimmed. A boy, pretending to be a wounded soldier, came in from outside. He was wearing a military uniform, limping and using a cane as he came down the aisle. It appeared to be an effort for him to slowly climb the three steps to the stage. He limped across the stage to an Army cot, dropped his cane to the floor, lay down on the cot and went to sleep.

In a moment, a bright star shone in a window across the stage from the cot. As the star moved toward the center of the stage, a curtain opened in the back part of the stage. There were shepherds watching the star. A child's voice, coming from offstage told the shepherds to "Fear not, for behold I bring you good tidings of great joy, which shall be to all people..." The children's chorus sang "Joy to the World."

The soldier boy slept on, while his classmates recited the scripture about the birth of the Christ Child and sang the appropriate Christmas carols. As the last verse of "Silent Night" was heard drifting away, the soldier boy awoke, rubbed his eyes, picked up his cane and limped slowly up the aisle and out into the winter night.

There was no applause after that pageant, only a reverent stillness. This was wartime and many servicemen would not be home for

CHRISTMAS. December 8, 1987

Little Tot Says His Christmas Piece Loud And Clear

Practice for the 1958 Christmas pageant at our local Baptist Church was under way. Our two older sons were to participate. I sat a row behind the children with our youngest son, Greg. It was

14

the Christmas season before Greg's third birthday in March.

One by one the children went to the stage to practice their pieces. Greg observed for a while then whispered, "Mommy, I want to say a piece, too!"

"You are just a little fellow, you are only 2!"

At that he loudly announced, "But I'm big enough!" The program director asked Greg what the problem was, and he told her. She humored him by telling him to practice at home and she would add his name to the program. Privately she told me a 2-year-old would not perform when the time came.

The night of the pageant the children went to the stage by turn to say their little poems. Some forgot their lines and had to be prompted, some spoke too softly and couldn't be heard, others repeated their lines so hurriedly it was difficult to understand. When all had finished, the director asked Greg if he'd like to come up and say his piece.

Greg slid off his father's lap, walked confidently up the steps and turned to face the audience. He planted his little feet squarely in center stage. A hush fell over the congregation. In a voice loud and clear, he began:

"I'm just a little fellow.

You see, I'm only 2 (held up two fingers),

But I'm BIG ENOUGH to wish a Merry, Happy Christmas to you!" (A pudgy forefinger scanned the crowd.)

Resounding applause broke out. Greg, grinning from ear to ear, joined the clapping. When the congregation quieted, the minister asked Greg to say the piece again to finish the program, and he did. Brother Bob scooped Greg up, carried him off the stage and deposited him with us, saying, "Folks, you heard his first performance in the Baptist church."

By his early teens, Greg was an accomplished pianist and performed many times in that same church. He became a professional musician, and we have attended many of his performances, but none sweeter than that long ago Christmas

PAGEANT. December 8, 1987

Everything Went Fine At Program Rehearsals

It was time for the Christmas program at our school, and the teacher had asked me to narrate the story of the birth of Christ. As I read, my classmates would enact it on the stage. We rehearsed several times and everything went fine.

My mother made me a beautiful navy blue dress with a red belt for the program. I felt very confident and dressed up. As I walked out to the front of the stage, I discovered that the teacher had set up a microphone. We had not included a microphone in rehearsals. To make matters worse, its volume had been set too high. Everyone jumped as my voice suddenly boomed out into the auditorium filled with friends and neighbors. The sound of my voice made me very nervous, and I developed a bad case of stage fright. Then the microphone gave a high-pitched squeal, and most of the audience covered their ears.

This was just too much for me. I began to giggle. The sound of my laughter over the microphone made things worse. I could not stop laughing! Every sentence I read was punctuated by my nervous giggles. Somehow I got through the Christmas story as my classmates acted out their parts.

Once it was over, I went backstage, and my laughter turned to tears of shame. I felt I'd ruined what could have been a beautiful program, all because of the unexpected
MICROPHONE. December 4, 1984

Pageant Without A Star

When my son was in kindergarten he was in a Christmas program at church. Our minister's wife was his teacher.

Four little 5-year-old boys were supposed to hold cards spelling STAR, a letter on each card. They practiced going up on one side of the stage, but the night of the program they went up the opposite side.

Four little boys, looking so proud, held up their cards spelling RATS. The audience had quite a chuckle, but the teacher's face turned
RED. December 8, 1987

Kids Put On Christmas Program For Small Town

It was almost Christmas in our small railroad town. There was no church and we wanted some sort of worship service. I asked my sister, "Don't you think we could have a program?"

"How? No place, no books for poems and plays," came her discouraging answer.

"We can make up poems and plays," I said, not giving up.

We got busy and planned a drill for nine children holding letters spelling Christmas. We made letters from wallpaper and cardboard, painting them red and green.

Angel wings were no problem with silver and white wallpaper. When the cheesecloth didn't hide the angel's long-sleeved underwear, we borrowed a white nightie.

The play we wrote was about an invalid woman who was showered with homemade gifts from children. For practicing, we used the barn, so Dad wouldn't have to stand the gaff.

Mother offered to play the accompaniment. Being a music teacher, she was really the only qualified person on our team. It was old hat for her to cover up mistakes, hesitations and off-key notes.

There was one problem left. Where would we have the play? Our neighbor heard about our play and said, "You kids can use my house."

The sliding doors were opened, and the dining room became our stage, with the living room for the audience. Benches and chairs were borrowed from homes and the pool hall.

All the town turned out. The kids performed better than they had in any of the rehearsals. At the end we asked everyone to join in singing "Joy to the World." Everyone complied, rendering a song as the shepherds must have heard that clear night.

The next day, Mary stopped to say, "The people from my church said you gave a better program than they."

Never has there been a Christmas like that one, and we were only 9 and 10 years

OLD. December 8, 1987

17

Eyesight For Santa

The Wise Men and the shepherds had left the scene. The lights came on and the Sunday School superintendent faced a large audience. More than 200 children looked at him with expectation. Now was the time—the time for Santa to appear!

In the pastor's study about 50 feet away were three frantic men. Word had come that the program was over, and now the sound of Santa's bells should be heard approaching the church. One man was crawling on the chairs and window seats and behind radiators. Another was picking up clothing and going through pockets and pulling out drawers in panicky haste. The third man, none other than Santa himself, was clawing his beard and protesting, "But I can't go in until I find them. I'd fall on my face without them!"

There was a knock on the door. Another man entered and asked why Santa was delayed. To his excited questions, Santa replied, "I must have my glasses! I've lost my glasses!"

The messenger began laughing. He reached up and pushed Santa's glasses onto his face, and the jolly saint went into his
ACT. December 20, 1955

Heard "Dimpled Darling" Too Often

It's funny, but I well remember a poem I recited in school 60-odd years ago when I was in the primary grades. The title was "Baby's First Christmas."

It began, "Hang up the baby's stocking, be sure you don't forget, for the dear little dimpled darling has never seen Christmas yet." There was another verse or so, then this conclusion: "I know what I'll do for baby, I've thought of a first-rate plan. I'll borrow a stocking from Grandma, the longest that ever I can. And you shall hang it by mine, dear, close by the chimney so Santa can fill it with goodies, from the top, right down to the toe."

The recitation must have had a very good reception the first time I gave it on a program, for I kept giving it week after week when we had Friday afternoon "speakings." The places on these programs were all filled by volunteers. Whether for a song, a recitation or a story, I always volunteered and always gave the same thing, until one Friday afternoon. Before I got through the first verse everybody was laughing. The teacher thumped his desk with a ruler, and I turned red-faced and tried to keep from crying as I went back to my seat.

I never recited that poem again, and you can believe I knew a new recitation before I volunteered to take part in a Friday afternoon speaking

AGAIN. December 11, 1979

Tiny Tot Ad-Libbed

I wasn't 2 years old until March, but in December they gave me a part in the Christmas program. My line was, "I'm glad for Jesus and his gentle love." My dad was quite a funny guy, so he taught me to say, "I'm glad for Jesus and his boxing gloves." My mother was afraid I'd say that so she sent me to the program with friends. She and Dad came later and sat in the back of the church.

I got up, said my piece and looked over the crowd. Just as I finished, I spotted Dad. I stuck my tongue out at him and said, "Blah, blah, blah!" The audience roared.

When Santa Claus gave out the treats, he handed me a sack of goodies and said, "Frances, I don't know if you need a treat after that performance." I gave it back to him and said, "Keep it. I have lots of good candy bars and pop at

HOME." December 2-9, 1975

Each Class Represents A Country

The nuns at our parochial school went all out when it came to the Christmas pageant. One year—perhaps when I was in the fifth grade—each class was going to represent a different country, putting on a show for the Christ Child. In my class, we were to be Dutch children.

We all learned dances from our countries. I envied the older

19

girls who were learning Irish and Scottish jigs and reels. We Dutch children danced to waltz time: stomp, clop, swish, swish.

Our mothers made us elaborate costumes out of crepe paper. We wore long blue skirts with little white aprons. Somewhere they found wooden shoes for us.

All went well until the big performance. It was hard to kick, swish-swish and hang on to wooden shoes. More than one shoe flew out over the stage. Then someone stepped on my long skirt. I heard the paper rip and grabbed a handful of pleats, hanging on until we were finished.

The finale was always the manger scene. Live children were supposed to hold their positions perfectly still without blinking an eyelid. This was hazardous because the tension often made one feel faint. One year parents with a new baby allowed the child to represent the Christ Child. However, the baby was not quiet, waving its little arms and cooing. The "statues" started giggling. That year we had an animated manger

SCENE. December 20, 1988

Beautiful "Silent Night"

One Christmas season, my husband and I were providing musical entertainment at a nursing home. As my husband played the violin, and I the piano, the room soon filled with handicapped men and women in wheelchairs. They sang songs with us.

Then the program director led a little, thin, blind woman to the piano. She wore a faded housecoat and house shoes. The director asked if she could sing "Silent Night" with us. I played softly as this dear woman sang the most beautiful soprano we had ever heard. When she finished, tears were streaming down her face.

She said, "Please let me sing again." The whole room applauded their consent.

Later we learned she had been a professional singer in her youth.

"Silent Night" will always mean more to me in the

FUTURE. December 22, 1987

20

Little One Lets It All Out

One Christmas pageant I will never forget is the one I saw when I went back home with my four sons to attend the church I had gone to so often.

Mom, Dad, my sons and I went to church for the program. The little ones were all so sweet, dressed in their best, faces shining. I bought my 4 1/2-year-old son, Mike, a little sailor suit. With his blond hair and blue eyes he looked like an angel.

The little ones finished their songs. Then all but Mike quietly left the stage. Mike looked all around, gave a yell like Tarzan, pounded on his chest and jumped off the stage! There wasn't a dry eye in church that night. Everyone was trying not to laugh, so tears ran down their faces. The woman playing the piano tried to play and wipe her eyes at the same time. As for me, I just wanted a place to

HIDE. December 22, 1987

Christmas Story Presented In Slides

My daughter, the Sunday School children, their parents and others in their church made slides of the Christmas story.

The children were dressed in bathrobes, sheets, drapes, etc.—whatever they could come up with for costumes. They took the photos at their farm in Iowa. Mary rode on a small pony while some of the other travelers rode on horses or walked.

When the angel appeared to the shepherds, they staged it on a rocky hillside, with the angel standing on an outcropping of rock above the shepherds and their sheep.

Other scenes were done with the same careful concentration on detail. All the children were pictured in some of the scenes.

The night the program was presented, the children sat on the floor in darkness so they could see the slides as they were shown. Each class took their turn singing as the slides were shown. It was so simply yet beautifully done. When the last slide came on the screen, it was so beautiful and moving. Mary and Joseph stood by the manger, which contained a live baby. There were sheep and

other animals in the background. A beautiful shaft of natural sunlight came from above, softly illuminating their expressive faces while the children sang "Away in a Manger" and "Silent Night." As the lights came up, more than one person in the audience was seen wiping away a tear or two. This was the best program
EVER. December 8, 1987

Needs A New Dress For School Christmas Pageant

My granddaughter just stopped by and left some beautiful red material and a pattern for me to make her a dress to wear at her school Christmas program. There will be 10 girls dressed alike, and they will sing the songs in the pageant.

This made me remember an incident that happened when I was 12 years old. We lived in a small town in the 1930s. My father was out of work, sometimes for weeks at a time. Because of my mother's creativity and ability to stretch pennies, we six children were never hungry, although many times a meal consisted of biscuits and gravy. With the help of a woman I'll call Aunt Mary—and the old garments and materials she had in her attic—we were adequately clothed for school and church.

Well, Christmas was drawing near. I was one of eight girls selected to sing a beautiful song for the Christmas program at our church. Four were then selected to sing one verse as a solo, and I was one.

My mother was delighted, but she and I knew most of the girls would either have a new dress or would be wearing what we called a Sunday dress. I just wore to church what I wore to school. This bothered me, but I said nothing about it, as a new dress was impossible.

Aunt Mary always gave each member of the family a new pair of stockings as a Christmas gift, so I knew I would have nice stockings to wear. We truly appreciated these gifts.

One day Aunt Mary brought over some gray material. It had a little luster to it and was enough to make me a pretty skirt, but I had no blouse to wear. Again Aunt Mary came to the rescue. She found a pale, cream-colored voile blouse and sewed some white buttons down the front. The blouse was nice, but the color did not go well against the gray.

Mother and I were looking at them when my little sister came into the room with a bit of red crepe paper in her hand. Her fingers were red from the paper. Mother asked her where she found the paper and she said at the Lodge Hall trash barrel. This gave Mother an idea. She sent me with a note to one of the lodge members asking if we might have the streamers. Permission was given and the streamers collected.

The next day the red streamers were put in a pot of hot water to boil the dye out. Then Mother put the blouse in the water. When I came home from school, I found a pretty pink blouse hanging with my gray skirt. Even the white buttons had become a shade of pink!

When we sang on Christmas Eve, a very happy girl wearing a gray skirt and pink blouse stepped forward to sing her
VERSE. December 9, 1986

CHRISTMAS WITH KATE

December Journeys

Chapter 3

*E*VEN THOUGH THERE'S no place like home for the holidays, in our fast-paced world, many of us find ourselves spending Christmas away from home and loved ones. Sometimes our jobs keep us away, sometimes it's the service. Even Mother Nature has been known to put a wrench in our plans to be home at Christmas.

Here are some stories that readers have shared with me about being both home and abroad during this special time of year. These tales of unexpected visits from loved ones, friends who keep in touch despite the miles, and discovering newfound Christmas spirit in the most unlikely of situations are sure to set your heart aglow.

Two Times $12.85

Six years ago we had saved for several months to take a trip home at Christmas. It had been necessary to save our expense money a little at a time, and we had it all saved when a minor accident took away $12.85 for the doctor and drug store. Of course, there would be a check coming at the first of the month, but that didn't help much right then—especially our feelings.

It was early afternoon, but we decided to eat a little lunch and go window shopping. Then the mail carrier's whistle sounded and somehow I knew our trip was on. As I raced for the mail, I called, "Get ready, we've only 35 minutes to catch the train."

The first letter I saw looked like an ad from the local store, but it had an overcharge slip amounting to $1.85. There was a dollar check from *Capper's*, a $5 bill from my husband's boss for his Christmas present and a $5 bill that we never expected to get back from a fellow who had borrowed it the Fourth of July. Did we catch the train? I'll say we did—and found there were rates that amounted to $12.85 off on our tickets! We divided the $12.85 and put it in savings for our two kidlets.

TWELVE EIGHTY-FIVE. December 20, 1930

Snow Almost Stops Christmas Festivities

When I was a child, four neighboring families took turns having Christmas. This consisted of a huge noon meal followed by a gift exchange. Later, there would be plates of homemade candy and cookies—the very thought made my mouth water.

Snow began the 23rd of December. "If it doesn't get any worse, we'll be able to make it," my mother reassured. Unfortunately, the 24th brought more snow, and by evening our narrow country roads were blocked by high drifts. I went to sleep praying the snowplow would come during the night.

Christmas morning dawned clear and cold. There was the usual stack of Santa Claus gifts under the tree. At breakfast time I mentioned the snowplow. "Even if he works today, he'll be expected to do the main roads first," my dad reminded me.

My mother sadly went to the phone to tell Mrs. Sheeks we couldn't come. Then she started working in the kitchen, trying to put together some sort of holiday meal.

Minutes later the phone rang. Mrs. Sheeks told Mother, "Ben can come for you through the fields in his Jeep. Only the east-west roads are blocked."

How well I remember the ride through the snow-covered fields that Christmas Day! The little house was filled with friends, laughter and warmth. The day lived up to my expectations in every way—with a big dinner, pretty gifts and an array of goodies.

All too soon it was dusk and chore time. Ben drove us home through the snowy fields as the first bright stars appeared in the darkening sky. It was a Christmas Day to
REMEMBER. December 18, 1984

Surprised Parents Christmas Eve

Of all the Christmases in the past, one especially stands out. Our parents lived in California, but we three children and our families lived in Kansas. We decided it would be fun to surprise our parents and all go to California for the holiday.

We met at a central point in Kansas. There were 16 of us in three cars. We drove straight through, often eating while traveling. The adults took turns driving. We had a feather bed in our station wagon so we could stretch out to rest.

Our youngest daughter worried, fearing Santa would not find her at Grandma's house. My husband and I smiled at each other, knowing that desired doll was riding along just above her head on the station wagon carrier.

We arrived on Christmas Eve. Pasadena was glittering with lights and beautiful decorations. We slowly approached our parents' home. Our arrival was unnoticed, so we gathered on the porch to sing a carol. Mother opened the door and excitedly called Dad. After all the weary hours of traveling, what a thrill to see the joy on their
FACES! December 8, 1981

Contagious Christmas

Christmas morning, 1944, I was a WAC stationed at Leyte, Philippine Islands. There morning was one of bright sunshine and palm trees, in contrast to the cold and snow of my Nebraska home. We had received no mail from home for many weeks and didn't know when we would get it.

I started to work as usual that morning, feeling homesick and alone. As I went through the gate to leave our area, I heard someone say, "Merry Christmas, Missy," and there stood a sweet little barefooted Filipino girl of about 10 years. With a smile lighting her whole face, she handed me a bunch of colorful native flowers. I was surprised, but her smile was so infectious that I smiled back, returned her cheery greeting and took the beautiful flowers.

As I walked briskly on to work, I felt happy inside. Christmas had somehow taken on new meaning for me. Entering the makeshift office where I worked, I shouted, "Merry Christmas, Sir," to my boss, an Air Force captain who was sitting at his desk looking as forlorn as I had felt earlier. I showed him the flowers and told him about the little girl. He said, "You know, for the first time in my life, I'm beginning to realize the true meaning of Christmas."

As others arrived at work, cheery greetings were exchanged, and Christmas in the Philippines wasn't so bad after all. Since that particular Christmas, I have remembered a sweet smile and cheery greeting as one of the nicest gifts I have ever
RECEIVED. December 25, 1956

Friends in Germany

My husband was in the Armed Forces stationed in Germany last Christmas. I had joined him in June, a bride of six months. Our Christmas began December 6, the children's St. Nicholas Day. St. Nick is the German Santa Claus, and through the efforts of our German landlady, he visited us, leaving candy and cookies.

On Christmas Eve we exchanged gifts beside a gift-laden table lighted only by a candle-lit potted tree. There was a moment of

28

silent thanks and then handshaking with each from whom a gift was received. A light supper followed. Then the radio was turned on, and we listened to a special Christmas music program given by the large churches.

After the gifts were displayed and our questions about their traditions answered, my husband and I returned to our tiny one-room apartment with our hearts full of feeling for the wonderful people who had taken us in on Christmas; to us they were not 'foreigners.'

We are in our own home now, and as Christmas draws near, we think of our German Christmas with fond
MEMORIES. December 17, 1957

Cabin Christmas In The Rockies

High in the Rocky Mountains in a cozy cabin is where I would spend Christmas if I had my wish. Snowbound in a deep silvery silence on the rooftop of the land with only my family; far from the crowds, commercialism and confusion, perhaps we could experience a pure Christmas without the tinsel and meaningless merrymaking.

I would have no television or radio, only a record player and some beautiful Christmas carols. No basketball or football games to crowd out the Christmas message. No office parties or gorges, no carnival stores, no perfunctory gift exchanges. A crèche, pine boughs and mugs of cocoa would be enough tradition.

In the ethereal peace of pine trees and snow-covered slopes, we would be closer to heaven, our hearts better prepared to wonder and rejoice in the birth of a
SAVIOR. December 19, 1972

Train Snowbound In A Christmas Blizzard

Our family was making a Christmas trip to California when our train was stopped out in the desert country of New Mexico. The wind was blowing a fierce gale, and they told us that a deep mountain cut ahead was filled with snow. We had to wait all day and far into the night before we could get through.

A passenger, who was a retired railroad engineer, helped "while away" the time for us by telling the story of his experience with a Christmas Eve blizzard. He had been the engineer on a little cut-off train that connected lines from the West Coast with a line to Denver.

One Christmas Eve he had five passengers, including a pregnant woman and her 3-year-old daughter. The woman's husband was going overseas, and she had stayed with him on the coast until he left.

The train was stopped at a little mountain station because a big cut ahead was filled with snow. They had no idea how soon it would be opened, and the passengers were stuck at the isolated station. That's when the young woman began to sob that she had waited too long to start back home—her baby was going to be born where there was no help, no doctor!

The blizzard was fierce by then, but the station agent told the woman not to worry because Aunt Molly and Uncle Jim lived only a half-mile away, and Aunt Molly was the best midwife within a hundred miles. He asked for volunteers to go to Uncle Jim's to get a horse and buggy to carry the woman there. The men who waded through the storm wrapped gunny sacks around their feet and legs, tied themselves together and made walking sticks. They gave the train whistle a toot before they left, so Uncle Jim and Aunt Molly knew something was up and had hot coffee ready for them when they arrived.

Uncle Jim hitched up old Charley and walked beside him to keep the buggy in the road. The passengers, including a banker and his wife from Denver, all accompanied the buggy bearing the suffering woman back to Aunt Molly.

Aunt Molly had a warm bed ready, and before morning an eight-pound boy was born. Uncle Jim was given the privilege of naming him and called him Joseph, after the son he and Aunt Molly had lost.

After the baby was born, there came the problem of feeding so many people. The banker told Uncle Jim he would replenish his larder if he would feed them. The old couple had a pen of hens, so the banker's wife cooked two chickens, baked dried apple pies, fried doughnuts and made a big pan of biscuits.

It was three days before the engineer and his passengers were rescued. The banker made good on his word, and the first train back included a coop of chickens and what looked like a small grocery store. He also invited them all to have Christmas dinner with him and his wife in Denver the next year.

The passengers parted with a warm spot in their hearts for Aunt Molly and Uncle Jim and vivid memories of a certain Christmas
EVE. December 21, 1954

Took Christmas To Texas Motel

I would not have believed it if anyone had told me I would enjoy being 800 miles from home on Christmas. But last year I did.

About a week before Christmas our youngest son, 18, who was stationed in Texas, called us and said he could not come home for Christmas. However, he would have four days off-duty, and could we come down? We had not seen him for several months, and it was his first Christmas away from us. We made our plans, and two days before Christmas loaded the car with gaily wrapped gifts, homemade cookies, candy, fruitcake and even a tree made from popcorn, and set out for Texas.

We picked up our son and one of his buddies who could not go home and moved into a motel, where we spent four glorious days. We decorated the motel and just had a grand time. On Christmas Eve we went to the base chapel for midnight mass. On Christmas Day we opened packages and enjoyed homemade goodies.

One week after we arrived home, our oldest son's wife presented us with our first grandson. Wasn't it nice of the stork to wait until we got home?

This year our Air Force son will get to come home, and we will have Christmas at home with all of our
CHILDREN. December 3-10, 1963

Trip to Mexico

My Christmas wish would be a trip to Mexico. We have a son working there, and his job will end about January 1, 1969. He has asked us often to come visit him, but living with a family on a farm we don't have much time for an extended trip.

So many say we should go while we have our own guide who speaks both English and Spanish. They celebrate Christmas so differently from the way we do. It would be an interesting time of year to take a

VACATION. December 3, 1968

Friends Get Together

The holidays will have a special meaning this year when three of my friends and I celebrate our 25th consecutive Christmas Eve together. We have food, share gifts and take pictures. It's so much fun to look at the pictures and see how our families have changed; all of our children have little ones now. They will all be with us this year to help us celebrate.

We have stood by one another through joys and sorrows, and we all know the others will stand by us if needed.

All of us are approaching 65 and can't expect to be together another 25 years, but we plan to aim for it

ANYWAY. December 7, 1982

Drifts Close Roads and Cover Fences For Christmas

The skies were gray and sullen the morning of December 24, 1919. Snow was beginning to fall and swirl around as the wind caught it. "Looks like it could be a blizzard," Papa said. "There was a ring around the moon last night." Mama came over to the window. "That's a sure sign," she agreed.

My heart sank. Tomorrow was Christmas, and we were to go to Grandma McConnell's. "Oh, please, dear God, let us go to Grandma's," I prayed.

My little sister Kathryn and I dressed in front of the oven door , trying to keep warm. All day the snow fell and the wind piled it in big drifts. Mama went ahead and made the pies. The snow kept falling. A real Kansas blizzard!

December 25, our big day! The sun shone, making a world of drifts and sparkles. The storm had gone on to Missouri, but we were snowbound. While eating our hot oatmeal and homemade bread, the party line rang the emergency signal. Mama answered, and a voice said, "Folks, you'll have to stay home today. The roads are all drifted shut. Merry Christmas!"

I went to the window and looked out, then the tears came. Our presents were at Grandma's.

Papa dressed in his boots and warm coat and went outside. When he came back, he said, "I've been looking at the old sleigh. I believe we can use it. It's only a couple of miles as the crow flies."

"What's 'as the crow flies,' Papa?"

"That is a straight line from here to Grandma's." Papa assured Mama the snow was pretty solid and frozen over the fence tops. We covered the pies and wrapped up as warm as we could, taking heavy lap robes. It was very exciting. Grandma and Grandpa and the relatives who had managed to get there met us at the door with "Merry Christmas" and lots of hugs. I could smell the goose roasting. Everything was wonderful.

Before long we could hear the sound of sleigh bells coming down the stairs, and there came Santa. He had a burlap bag over his back and red hair sticking out of his cap. We opened the sliding doors to the parlor, and there was the most beautiful tree and packages all around. After handing out packages Santa went up the stairs. After awhile our red-haired Uncle John came down the stairs. We then had a delicious Christmas dinner.

We had to go home early to do chores. When you go "as the crow flies," you don't want to take any chances.

I've remembered that Christmas for about 65 years. The memory never

DIMS. December 23, 1986

Ice Storm Changed Plans For Holiday

Christmas in Springfield, Missouri, was very different in 1987. A terrific ice storm caused the power to go off in many parts of the city. Three of our children were with their in-laws. The power went off in all three homes, and they came to our house earlier than expected. We gathered around the tree and read Luke, Chapter 2, prayed and sang carols.

Suddenly one of the children suggested we open our gifts right then and there. By midnight of Christmas Day, we were just about finished opening our gifts, and it was a good thing. Our power went off about 5 a.m. We have a fireplace, but couldn't keep the house warm enough for children 2 months, 6 months and 3 years old.

We have a son and daughter who live in town. The son got called in to work, and we didn't see him at all that day. They live in a three-room apartment, but they had heat, so we all went to her home for our Christmas dinner. Fortunately, I had cooked the turkey the day before. We boxed everything I had prepared. Our daughter called twice, once to ask us to bring more forks and the second time to bring more toilet tissue.

My husband went out to warm the car, and a stranger asked him if the wood out back was ours. The man's 83-year-old grandmother lived with them, and they had no heat except the fireplace. We filled his station wagon with firewood.

We did manage to put together a nice dinner and have a wonderful time in that tiny kitchen. There were 11 of us, plus three birds in large cages that she was keeping for a friend. We spent most of the afternoon loving babies and playing Pictionary.

In the afternoon we discussed where to sleep everyone in this one-bedroom apartment. However, the power was restored about 6 p.m. As soon as our house warmed we went home, but many people were without power for
SEVERAL DAYS. December 6, 1988

The Season Of Giving

Chapter 4

SOME SAY THAT Christmas is "just for kids."
But everybody from the tiniest tot to good
old Dad loves to find a gift under the tree
for them. Some yearn for the doll in the store window, others for just one impractical pair of fuzzy
slippers. Those who are alone for the rest of the
year simply hope to be remembered.

My readers have given and received countless
gifts over the years—here's a sampling of just a
few. Some were homemade, some store-bought;
all were given with love. If you've run out of
ideas, these letters may provide you with the
gift-giving inspiration you need for someone
special on your list.

Granny Wants Fuzzy Slippers And Perfume

Christmas is just around the corner. I know all wonder what to give dear old Grandma, so I am going to give you a few pointers.

Please, not another "nice, warm sweater" or poncho. My closet is so full I can hardly get the door closed. One of these days, if I am so lucky as to be left home alone, I am going to pack them all in a big carton and get Jim, the handyman next door, to take them to that old ladies' home down in the village.

Clara, could you possibly find a pair of those pretty fuzzy bedroom slippers in my size? I am so tired of those drab knitted kind that stretch out of shape in a week and won't stay on my feet.

Maude, how about forgetting about the assortment of hard candies and get me a box of nice, soft chocolates, the kind with the gooey cherries inside.

Eloise, why don't you forget about your rose water-and-glycerin hand lotion and get me a box of good-smelling bath powder or a bottle of alluring perfume?

Marge, I know you are busy sewing for all your grandchildren, so why don't you skip my granny nightie this year and get me one of those flimsy nighties? Preferably in red with one of those things you wear over them—I can't remember the name, but it sounds something like pregnant.

I hope I am not asking too much of you, my dear family. I am looking forward to enjoying this Christmas, for next year I will be 80 and will have to be

SENSIBLE. December 17-24, 1974

Secret Gift Adds Christmas Fun

I was 12 when it started. I wanted a doll for Christmas. It had been years since my parents had given me a doll. They believed in a practical Christmas, with useful gifts, such as clothes. That year my mother gave me my Christmas spending money, and for the first time allowed me to select the gifts. Of course, she admonished me to "get something useful."

I did. But I snitched just a little from each gift, so that I had enough left for the cherished doll. I wrapped it in an old parcel wrapping that still had canceled stamps on it, and pasted a piece of paper over the address with my name and "Your Secret Pal" as the sender.

On the Saturday before Christmas I brought it in with the rest of the mail. While there were some remarks about the sender's identity, the gift's foolishness and me being "too old for dolls," nobody suspected the truth.

Since then that secret pal has sent me something every Christmas, and it's always something frivolous that no member of my family would ever dream of giving me. Once it was costume jewelry, once some lovely lingerie, occasionally a book or record I really wanted and once a lovely little music box.

This bit of deception has added a lot of fun to my Christmas shopping, and it is always a pleasure to know that I am going to find at least one gift under the tree that I

REALLY WANT. December 19, 1972

Her Heart Beat Like A Steam Engine

When I was just a little girl, a beginner in our little country school, we had an evening Christmas program with a tree all lit up with candles. Best of all, our teacher said Santa Claus might make a visit. I was wearing a red merino dress trimmed with lace at the neck and sleeves that my mother had just finished for me.

The teacher was right about Santa. He came even before the program started, not down the chimney, which was almost red-hot from the fire in the pot-bellied stove, but through the window. He had a big sackful of toys and goodies. These he piled around the tree with its lovely blazing candles. Suddenly I spied a doll, a lovely doll with curls and a red merino dress just like mine—even lace around the neck and sleeves. Could it be for me? I could think of nothing else. I wanted that doll more than anything in the world. Fortunately, my part in the program was just the littlest angel with only a few words to say.

After the program Santa began to hand out the gifts: first the

37

sacks of goodies, then gifts for the little preschoolers. When he picked up the doll with the red dress, my heart was beating like a steam engine. He held it up as if in doubt about who should have it. He looked past me and over the whole roomful, even the great big girls. I suddenly felt like crying and the tears were already starting when he looked back at me and said, "Why, here's a little girl with a red dress just like this doll's. I am sure the doll should go to her."

Suddenly I was the happiest little girl, if not in the whole world, at least in that little schoolhouse. Of course, I gave Santa all the credit for both the doll and the red dress that just matched mine. It was several years later that I understood and appreciated my mother's love and work. To this day, I still like red

BEST. December 17-24, 1974

Too Much Christmas

Don't dazzle your children with too much Christmas. They don't demand so much. It is the relatives who enjoy buying the extravagant gifts and an oversupply of them.

I remember the year Charlotte was 3. We were at her grandfather's house, and because she was the only child in the family everybody sort of "turned loose." With three uncles and two aunts, the grandparents and her daddy and me, we really put on a Christmas for Charlotte. The tree reached the ceiling and was ablaze with lights. The toys piled beneath would have started a toy store. There was a train and track and a little auto she could ride in, three new dolls, trunks and dishes, little toy furniture, blocks and books and a plush bear on wheels. Someone bought a little doll swing, and because it needed a doll in it, I picked up Charlotte's old favorite, "Pink." Now "Pink" was worn and bedraggled but fit in the swing, and it didn't show much under the branches.

Well, the big moment finally arrived. It was Christmas morning, and the audience was in place when Charlotte was brought in to see what Santa Claus had done for her. Such a little girl in front of the big wonderland that was her family's interpretation of

Christmas! She stood speechless before the bright glitter. "What will she pick up first?" someone whispered, hoping it might be his gift. Presently she moved toward the marvelous display. Then reaching out her arms for her old dolly she said happily, "There's Pink."

BONNIE. December 22, 1945

Fresh From The Farm

Those of us who are farmers may feel we cannot give this year. But if we feel that way—we are wrong—for we have right at hand a wealth of good things to eat—which are doubly welcome in the city.

Look over your jellies, jams, preserves, marmalades, pickles and relishes. In small containers, these are welcome additions to a holiday breakfast or luncheon. Mincemeat, canned fruit, carrots, even potatoes are welcome if clean.

Little odd-shaped jars of real country whipping cream will bring you heartfelt thanks from those who must buy this luxury. Pats of country butter, cottage cheese and cream cheese add a new and festive note to any holiday box. With eggs sky-high, any cook will be more than grateful for a carefully packed dozen.

Dressed fowls are often the answer to a big worry in some hard-pressed housekeeper's heart. Perhaps she has been trying to figure out how to stretch money far enough to buy one.

All children will love bags or stocking made of gay cloth and filled with popcorn. Dry beans, wheat and nuts are not to be scorned. Home-ground cornmeal or cracked wheat is another idea. If you are fortunate enough to have honey, that is indeed a golden gift. Cakes, pies and cookies are well-known and oft-given gifts.

Home-made soap can be attractively wrapped and is sure to prove a boon to the thrifty housewife who must buy such things. Before you decide that you cannot give—look about you. Perhaps you have something you can share after all.

SILVER BELLS. December 15, 1934

Thought Santa Might Miss Her

It was 1931. Mama, Daddy, we three kids, two unmarried uncles, an aunt and her husband all lived with Grandma and Grandpa in their four-room house. Nobody could find a job. We burned wood, had a cistern, coal-oil lights and ate homegrown corn, bread and black-eyed peas. The gallon of milk from Old Jersey was saved for the children and used in bread and gravy.

I was 6 and couldn't believe Santa would miss me as Grandma said he might. All the grownups loved and cared for us children. We didn't feel unimportant or neglected.

In December, Daddy got three weeks work picking cotton. It paid 50 cents a day, and he had to walk 12 miles to get there. He took along a skillet and quilt and slept out. We needed so many things, and Grandma continued to tell me Santa would probably miss our house.

Dinner was planned. We would have the old speckled rooster with dressing, sweet potato pie and crack some hickory nuts and pecans Grandma had been saving.

Christmas morning I was filled with joy to find a tiny red-headed doll for me, a little red truck and a rattle for my brothers. There was a sack of hard candy for everyone. Grandma kept talking about how foolish a father was who would spend a day's pay for a youngun's toy when we needed so many things, but I caught her looking at me with my dolly and smiling

ALL DAY. December 18-25, 1973

Clever Old Grandma

Every year Grandma S. drags out the scrap bag and proceeds to make gifts for one and all. The cost is usually almost nothing, but believe it or not, so clever are her gifts all of us wait eagerly to see what shall be ours from the old scrap bag.

Aprons are made from feed and flour sacks, in clever patterns, trimmed with gay tape and prints. From the same sacks Grandma fashions luncheon sets, tablecloths, tea towels, laundry bags, pillow covers, quilted bath mats, show bags and underwear—not to mention the cutest doll clothes on land or sea!

From old stockings she makes braided rugs and mats. Sock dolls there are, too, wearing clever clothes. There will be other toys this year according to Grandma, who is being very secretive. Last year there were inner-tube animals—stuffed, of course. And she even fashioned and painted inner-tube mats to protect the table from hot dishes.

For the very young she had spool dolls and bibs. The bibs were in the shape of a rabbit's head, made of Turkish toweling so that they required no ironing.

And for the age which scorns a homemade gift, however fine, Grandma gave each a shining quarter, explaining—"I made it— canning fruits and selling them."

HOLLY. December 15, 1934

Secret From Daddy

We were living abroad, where intricate little German-made electric trains were quite reasonable in price. For some time we had discussed starting a collection for our 3- and 4-year-old sons. We hesitated, feeling if we didn't take advantage of the opportunity now we might regret it when we got back to the States.

The solution seemed rather obvious. Thinking this could develop into a family hobby, I suggested to the boys that instead of the expensive shotgun they wanted to get Daddy, they get him a train instead. It wasn't hard to convince them! The boys and I bundled up and hurried to purchase our gift. We picked out a set we thought Daddy would like, and all the way home we talked of how we three had a secret and wouldn't tell Daddy about the train; we'd take it in the house and hide it and be very careful that Daddy didn't find our secret.

Getting out of the car, we carefully hid the package among others and walked into the house. Our 3-year-old danced on ahead calling, "Daddy, Daddy—we bought you a train, but we're not going to tell you

OUR SECRET!" December 17, 1957

41

Teddy Bears Made From Jacket

In 1945, we had three little boys and not too much money for presents. The weather was bad, too, and I had no time or desire to get out in the cold. I sent to *Capper's Weekly* for a teddy bear pattern, then wondered what type material to use.

Before I was married, I'd bought a curly black imitation fur jacket. I really loved that jacket. As I looked at it, I could see two teddy bears with shiny button eyes. One day while the children napped, I cut them out. Then came the sewing and stuffing. Before the first one was done, the oldest boy had seen me working on it. Of course, he asked who it was for. I told him I thought I would help Santa. When finished I put the bear in a large paper sack on top of the cupboard. Each morning he would look to see if Santa had taken it.

Eventually, the other teddy bear was finished, sacked and placed beside the first one. There was enough "fur" material left to make a large-sized ball for the baby. It, too, went in a sack for Santa to give to some little child.

Christmas morning, when the boys found the teddy bears under their own tree, they were so happy that Santa decided to leave them there. Our second boy slept with his teddy bear for several years.

I never had any regrets about my
JACKET. November 30, 1976

Ten Pleased Quilters

Last Christmas—in a large department store—I saw boxes containing quilt pieces with a pattern that could be used to make a quilt. These boxes sold all the way from 50 cents to $3.50. It gave me an idea. I bought boxes at 5 cents each. When I came home, I went through my trunk and the scrap bags and hunted out pieces of dresses, etc., classified them as to color and wearing quality, then attached a quilt pattern to go well with the scraps. I bought a 10-yard bolt of solid-colored lavender at a cost of 10 cents a yard. Cutting it in yard lengths, I put a yard in each. I made up 10 boxes at a cost of 15 cents each and sent them to 10 friends who like to quilt. Boxes left from last Christmas will answer the purpose, and if you have your own scraps, the boxes may be filled at virtually no cost at all.

G.R. December 12, 1931

Aunt Emma's Aprons

Every Christmas I get a package from Aunt Emma. I always know what it will be, for Aunt Emma can be depended on!

I know it will be an apron, yet I can hardly wait to open her package, for Aunt Emma's aprons are dreams. Every year she spends a lot of time selecting new apron patterns. Through the year she buys colorful fadeproof prints. She has a rainbow selection of tapes and organdy.

I don't mind telling you there are folks who would give their eyeteeth for one of those creations she turns out. Brides dream about wearing them; women in their 40s grow gay in them; and as for me, I'm wondering these days just what kind Aunt Emma will send this year.

APRON ALICE. December 15, 1934

Gift For Bird Lover

A little old lady who lives alone gets so much enjoyment out of feeding birds at her dining room window that a neighbor gave her a "bird cake" as a gift. It was made by melting tallow, then mixing it full of grain and various kinds of seeds and crumbs. The mixture had been put in a flat pan to cool, and when cold and solid it had been removed and enclosed in a 10-cent toaster. The toaster was decorated in keeping with the season and looked very bright and cheerful as it hung outside the window for the birds to feed. I'm sure the little lady enjoyed it much more than if it had been a cake for herself.

NEIGHBOR ANN. December 13, 1941

Gift Book To Be Sure

I have a small loose-leaf notebook, which I keep in a handy place along with a pencil. At the top of each page I write the name of one of my family or friends. Every time I hear one of them say, "I'd sure like to have so and so—" I write it down under their name in my little book. Then when Christmas or birthdays roll around I can look at my list and choose something to buy that I know they want. I could never remember until I started writing it down. When I'd hear someone mention something they wanted I'd think to myself, "Now, I must remember that," but when the time came I always forgot. Now the family has even started using my little book. When they want to buy a gift for someone they say, "Mom, where is your 'wants' book. I want to buy a gift for __." It's a good idea, and the best part of it is it works. Each time someone receives one of the things I have in my book I mark it off

MY LIST. December 7, 1946

Delivers Christmas Gifts Early

I just delivered my Christmas gifts! I have many friends who are shut-ins and others who are confined to nursing homes. Recently one of them told me she dreaded Christmas because it was so hard for her to write cards and letters (she has arthritis). She also mentioned it was hard for an older person to get out in cold weather and on icy sidewalks to buy a few cards.

I suddenly realized how difficult it was for these people to share the joy of Christmas. I bought each of them a box of Christmas cards (I ordered them from a card company). I stamped each envelope; I ordered name and address labels for each person. The cards, stamps and address labels cost less that $3 total per person.

I wish I could tell you the pleasure these people showed when I gave them their early Christmas gift.

My happiness was doubled. The gift was useful and welcome, and in turn these people would be able to spread Christmas cheer to

OTHERS. December 4-11, 1973

In Farm Wrappings

Here is a clever way to present gifts from the farm. Hollow a pumpkin. Fill the pumpkin with various farm products: jelly, butter, eggs, sausage, pickles; oh, you can think of many things! The pumpkin may later be used for pie. The person who originated this idea cut a door in the side of the pumpkin, drew a latch and hinges with ink and fastened the door with toothpicks.

MRS. E.E. RANKIN. December 17, 1932

Holiday Will Be Lonely

Christmas is going to mean heartaches at our house this year. You see, our Santa Claus is in the armed forces in Japan, and he won't be home for Christmas. Eight years ago he wasn't home for Christmas, either. He spent that one in a German prisoner camp and received a half of one raw turnip for Christmas dinner.

Now he is working in an ammunition depot in Japan, and he hopes he will have to work Christmas Day so it will go faster. But it will be long for me, and I don't know how I'll stand it. Oh, Santa will come to our house. I couldn't disappoint the children, but my Christmas will be such an empty thing without my husband.

If you are feeling sorry for yourself because you can't afford a television set, have a thought for the boys and their wives and mothers who would gladly never receive another Christmas gift if we could only have our loved ones

HOME. December 20, 1952

To Hide A Gift

Do you have trouble hiding packages from your children? If so, just put them inside a pillowcase, pin the case to a coat hanger, and then cover it with a coat or robe and hang it in the closet.

If you have other favorite hiding places, I suggest you make a note of the articles and the places they are hidden. Prevents a house-wide search for hidden gifts on Christmas

EVE. December 1, 1970

Dolls For Grownups

Children are not the only ones who like rag dolls for Christmas. I have given several to grownups, and they go over in a big way. I made a pretty colonial doll with shining black braids and dressed her in a bright blue dress and poke bonnet and lacy pantalets. What a surprise it was for the dear friend who received it. Her appreciation was wholehearted when she told me, "I was 6 when I got my first doll and 60 when I got my next one." She keeps it sitting in the corner and shows it to children who come to call. She has told me many times how pleased she was to have the doll which she named "Penelope."

DOLL MAKER. December 15, 1945

Photos For Mom

If you're looking for a gift idea for a mother, here's a good one. Make a point of taking as many snapshots as possible of her children. Select the best, and put them in a small album that holds 20 pictures. This photographic record brings great pleasure for a small

EXPENSE. December 1, 1970

Ribbon 'N' Bell Harness

A ribbon harness is a fine gift for the little tot. Boys and girls play "horsey" by the hour with it. Three yards of bright red ribbon and a number of little bells make the harness. Allow one-half yard for each shoulder strap and the rest for the chest and reins, making loops at the ends of the reins. Sew bells across the chest strap.

PEGGY. December 6, 1941

Stamp Books For Boys

Five years ago my sister, who always has the Christmas spirit no matter how flat her pocketbook, made each of her six nephews a scrapbook containing about a hundred canceled stamps. The boys lived many miles apart in four different states and ranged in ages from 6 to 15 years. But their stamp collections formed a club among them, and they each have a stamp collection in their boy groups where they live. My son's collection has grown until it contains more than a thousand stamps and has helped him more in his geography lessons than any other one thing. Pre-cancels from the different states have given him a fixed idea of that state. His foreign stamp collection has been the incentive for him to bring his geography home many times to look up locations. You might be surprised how many busy businessmen have taken an interest in him through his stamp collection and have saved stamps for him. It has given him something to occupy his mind and hands. I have surely thanked the day my sister spent the 15 cents she said it cost to buy loose-leaf notebook paper and glued hinges to start six stamp collections. It's the Christmas spirit and not money that makes the gift.

SISTER SUE. December 15, 1934

Not A Bit Too Young

I was washing dishes when my small 6-year-old suddenly inquired: "Mom, how much do men's garters cost?" Remembering that her Daddy had recently expressed that need, I was instantly on guard. "I'm afraid they cost a whole dime at least," I said. Her small brows contracted in disappointment.

"Mom," she asked a minute later, "how much do a man's and a lady's handkerchief cost?" And still later, "Do you like penny candy bars, Mom? Does Daddy like penny candy bars?" At my assurance that we just loved penny candy bars, she slipped away to count again the wad of pennies in the corner of a dirt-begrimed little kerchief.

"Heck," her Daddy said, "tell the little tyke not to worry about Christmas gifts!"

Should I? And deprive her of that grand satisfaction of experiencing that it is more blessed to give than receive? Oh, no! It is such a big lesson so grandly learned. Let her learn the joy of it now.

NELL. December 17, 1938

Made With Love

My one Christmas gift that will always be treasured is one I'd always wanted but didn't think I'd ever have. Not only for it, but because of the love with which it was given, I treasure it.

A few years ago my son surprised us with a new bedroom suite he had made himself. I wouldn't take any amount of money for it. It is better made than any bought set.

The suite has a bookcase bed, dresser, chest of drawers and night stand. I've always been very proud of it and have had many compliments on the set. I know our son put a lot of long, tedious hours—as well as love—into making the furniture, and we love him more

FOR IT. December 21-28, 1965

"Secret" Christmas Gift For Mother

It is quite an ordinary pink glass dish. The style was very common at the time I received it, ranging in price from 15 cents upward. This one is quite large and may have cost as much as 35 cents. I never use it, though, without remembering the evening that I first held it in my hands, trying my best not to look at it.

It was a Christmas present, meant to be smuggled into the house, then secretly placed under the tree. The day our little 7-year-old brought it home was cold and snowy. She had a half-mile walk up the hill from the school bus stop, with lunch pail and school papers to deal with besides the bulky, hard-to-handle package. By the time she got home the thin, red tissue-paper wrapping was torn in numerous places. Her tear-streaked face was scarlet from cold wind, her mittened hands about frozen.

As I hastened to help her with her things, she burst into fresh tears: "This is for you for Christmas, but I'm so cold I can't even care if you do guess what it is!"

I assured her I couldn't possibly imagine what such a big package could be and hurriedly placed it with the other gifts under the tree. Do you wonder that I cherish it after nearly 30

YEARS? December 7-14, 1965

Friendship's Music

Lottie, a good friend of mine, and I were discussing music boxes. She mentioned how, when younger, she'd hinted a number of times for a powder music box, but no one had ever given her one. I explained how I'd always adored the church music boxes. It seemed to me that it would be nice to have one to play, come Christmas, as it would bring something special to the home.

She answered that she'd looked at some church music boxes in a store, but because of some other expense, she couldn't afford one. In the meantime, I went about making a cardboard church—painting doors and windows—to use with my Christmas decorations. With a little patience and work I had a fairly good looking church.

Then, just before Christmas, in walked my friend carrying a little white church music box. She said, "Here's your church." I trembled as I took it in my hand, and tears came to my eyes as I said, "You bought one for me and you don't have one yourself."

She smiled and explained that it hadn't cost very much as it was broken. Her husband, who can weld, had fixed it so it would play again. While he mended, she prayed it would play again. So now I still treasure my church, and I treasure the good in hearts that made my Christmas dream

COME TRUE. December 22, 1953

Like An Angel Choir

The Christmas I held my premature, three-day-old baby boy in my arms was the most magical for me. That night, when the university carolers stopped to sing, it sounded to me like the Heavenly Host adding peace and joy to the blessed privilege of motherhood.

We lost our first-born son at birth 14 months earlier. Less than 18 months after that Christmas, I underwent surgery and could have no more children. The 10 doctors who watched the operation did not expect me to recover. They said it was a miracle that I had a strong, healthy youngster and was spared to raise him.

Our son is stationed in the Far East this Christmas, and we will be alone. He says not to worry, that he is well and all of his material needs are supplied. He writes often, and his airmail letters come in five days. Having a wonderful son is like a perpetual

CHRISTMAS. December 20, 1955

Baskets And A Little Paint

A lovely and useful present for someone may be made from a half-bushel fruit basket. Paint the slats cream and the hoops rose, or any combination you wish. For a hamper for baby's clothes, line the basket with rose-colored oil cloth. One little tot keeps his blocks and toys in a similar basket. There is no end to the possibilities of use in any household for one of these baskets.

ELIZABETH MORRISON. December 12, 1931

Grandmothers Should Write It Down

Are you a grandmother who does not know what to give her grandchildren for Christmas? I have a solution.

The best Christmas presents I ever gave my grandchildren were books of stories I had written about when their grandfather and I were children. I was amazed at what I remembered when I sat down to record events. Even my sons-in-law seemed excited over the stories.

If you can't write, get an inexpensive tape recorder and just record the stories. We underestimate the value of these folk tales passed down from generation to generation.

I tried to write about family members, our celebrations, where their ancestors came from and when, and, of course, some funny stories. I cut out Christmas pictures and pasted them on the front of the construction-paper covers, tied them with green and red yarn and they were ready.

I put names on the covers and special notes for each child. Though they are older now, they still talk about these books.

So, give your grandchildren some roots for

CHRISTMAS. December 6, 1988

"Doll" Receives One

This Christmas, joy really should have gone to my wonderful, thoughtful husband, although it brought tears of joy to the rest of the family. A year ago in January, our family was blessed with a baby girl—the first girl in our family in over 50 years. We have two wonderful grandsons and love them, too, but to say this girl was the apple of Grandpa's eye would be putting it mildly. He came to me one day when she was about 5 months old and said, "Here is some money. Would you go to town and get her a doll for Christmas? We can get the boys nice gifts later, but I want this put away for her Christmas."

I got the doll and put it away as he wished. Just before Christmas he passed away suddenly, so naturally we were all in shock. I was so thankful on Christmas morning that there was a box under the tree with this message, "A pretty baby for Grandpa's Doll."

Needless to say there were a few wet eyes. Somehow I hope Grandpa knew his wish had been
                    GRANTED. December 13, 1977

Letters To Santa

Each member of our family writes a letter to Santa and pins it to the bulletin board in the kitchen three weeks before Christmas. Maybe Mother would like a teapot to match her dishes; Dad may want some new camera equipment; Sister wants records. If pattern name, brands and sizes, names of records, etc., are included, Santa can bring just what is wished for. Our letters to Santa have been a big help in preventing disappointment at our
                    HOUSE. December 1, 1959

Package Of Her Own

A little motherless 8-year-old girl rode the same bus as my children to a rural school. She never looked as well-dressed as the other children, though the father did well to keep his children together.

51

Times were hard for all of us, but one Christmas I managed to get this little girl two dresses, some hair ornaments, and some underthings, all new. I met the bus one evening and poked the package through the window to the child. Not much was said, but I'll never forget how large her brown eyes got as she said disbelievingly, "Is it really for me?" No words could speak more thankfulness than that pair of big brown eyes in a
PALE FACE. December 14, 1954

Truly Personal Gift
A wonderful gift for the girl in the family who intends to get married is a friendship tablecloth for Christmas. I use red Indianhead and hem it neatly. Then I have her senior classmates or other friends sign their names on the cloth. I embroider the names in contrasting floss. I like green best, but a variety of colors is pretty.

In years to come when her friends have scattered, her holiday feasts can be shared with friends as she looks over her
FRIENDSHIP CLOTH. December 24, 1957

Deck the Halls

Chapter 5

CHRISTMAS JUST WOULDN'T be Christmas without the wreaths, ornaments and other decorative touches that make the home a special place during the holidays. Some holiday decorating traditions, such as electric tree lights, are relatively new. Others, such as wreaths, mistletoe and poinsettias, can be traced back for hundreds of years.

The following letters will remind you of decorations of the past. They will also give you new ideas for ways to make your home and gifts more festive. Add a little of your own imagination, and the possibilities are endless!

Dad Helps Us Decorate

We have lots of fun making decorations at our house—even Dad joins in the fun. As a centerpiece for our Christmas dinner table we use a mirror to represent an icy lake, surrounding it with evergreen boughs. Fat, jolly snowmen skate over its glassy surface. These are made of fluffy marshmallows. Take two for the legs, fasten them together with a toothpick. Set another marshmallow on these two for the snowman's middle. A fourth atop of this for his face. Next cut a marshmallow in halves, wet the edges and place one on either side of his middle for arms. Make hat and feet of colored gumdrops. Use cloves for eyes, nose and mouth. A sprinkle of artificial snow on the mirror adds a last realistic touch.

DECORATOR. December 14, 1935

Make Your Own Advent Wreath

Since the season of Advent begins four Sundays before Christmas, you might enjoy the ritual of lighting the traditional Advent wreath. It is a delightful pre-Christmas custom that allows a family to re-live the period of preparing for the coming of Christ.

To make an Advent wreath, use an eight- or nine-inch circle of green Styrofoam, intertwining it with small artificial leaves, similar to the leaves of a hedge. Punch four depressions into the wreath, and into these, place three purple candles of medium size. In the fourth depression, place a pink candle.

On the first Sunday of Advent, one purple candle is lit during the main meal of the day. The second purple candle, as well as the first, is lit the next Sunday of Advent. All three are lit on the third Sunday. Finally, the entire wreath is aglow, as the remaining pink candle is lit on the last Sunday of Advent, just before Christmas.

This is a time of joy and hope, and what more appropriate way can it be expressed than by the family gathering together at mealtime and lighting the colorful wreath of the Advent

SEASON. November 25, 1969

Our Tree Decorations

The candles on our tree are not real ones. We buy lots of short stick candy. Wrapping each one in white cellophane and giving a tight twist to one end, we paste a flame-shaped piece of red tissue paper in place and set them in the candle holders.

Cookie dough is baked in the shapes of trees, wreaths and stars and gaily decorated. A length of fine wire is strung through the top of each one and bent to hang on the Christmas tree.

Dad pops heaps of snowy popcorn, and we divide the syrup, coloring each part a different color. We mold each popcorn ball around some little surprise treat, then wrap it in white cellophane and attach a long string. These balls are heaped in the center of the table so they resemble a huge snowball. A string leads to each plate. After dinner each guest pulls a string, and the mass comes gaily tumbling down amid shouts of merry laughter.

MRS. B.N. December 14, 1935

Christmas Egg "Balls"

Christmas will soon be here, and I'd like to pass on to other mothers of tiny tots an idea I tried out last Christmas when we decorated our tree. We have two little boys who thoroughly enjoyed themselves coloring eggshells with Easter egg dye. (I found an obliging clerk in a dime store who rounded up a package for me.)

For several weeks before Christmas I "blew" the eggs I needed for cooking by tapping a hole in each end of the egg and then blowing through one end. I saved the empty shells, and when the boys had dyed them we waxed them. With a darning needle we ran bits of bright yarn through the shells, knotting one end and leaving a loop in the other.

These made very satisfactory "glass balls" and weren't a bit expensive when the temptation to "see if they'd bounce" became too great for a 2- and 3-year-old to resist. Our tree was decorated and redecorated many, many times, and the hours of pleasure they had were a source of pleasure to my husband and

TO ME. December 7, 1946

Lovely Holiday Table

If you are looking for an attractive holiday table arrangement, one that requires a minimum of time and expense—and looks like a million—perhaps you will like this idea. Spread a lovely white cloth on your table. Cut bands of red cellophane four to six inches wide—one for each place—and allow each to extend several inches below the table edge. Bring all together in the center of the table in a glistening bow, in the middle of which a tall, red candle may be placed. On the white cloth sprinkle—hit-and-miss fashion—the contents of a 10-cent box of assorted sizes of red stars. You will be proud to seat family or guests at this striking table.

DECORATOR. December 14, 1935

Christmas Balloons

Are your pretty tree decorations in danger because of small ones in the home? I found this idea displayed in the picture window of a local attorney's home. The tree was decorated with tinsel and balloons of all colors. So pretty! So practical, too, at least for lower

BRANCHES. December 4-11, 1973

Christmas Cones

Surprise the youngsters Christmas morning with candy hanging on the tree in these containers. Take old Christmas cards or bright wrapping, roll them into a funnel shape and glue together, then round off the tops and run a string through each to hang on the tree. They'll be handy to hold Santa's candy and nuts.

HELPING SANTA. December 11, 1948

Snowy Trees Are Fun

Small fry will love Christmas tree cones. First, tint some thawed frozen whipped topping to a pale green—just one drop of green will do it. Frost the outside of ice cream cones—the pointed kind—with the topping, and decorate with silver dragées and green sugar sprinkles. Top each with a star cut from a yellow gumdrop. Carefully place the tree on a slice of ice cream. Serve at once, or store in freezer.

Frost miniature doughnuts with pale green tinted topping and decorate with small gumdrops. These also may be served on ice CREAM. December 25, 1979

Colorful Burning Yule Logs Easily Made

Every year we make some of these logs for the fireplace and enjoy them through the holidays. We'd like to share the "recipe" so others can brighten their season.

Use a wooden container not bound by wire, as the acid will "eat" through other materials. Old newspapers and other absorbent papers should be rolled compactly to form logs about 16 inches long. Tie them with heavy twine, not too tightly, and soak in a solution made of one pint bluestone and five pints coarse salt. Put the bluestone in a cheesecloth over a container and pour boiling water until it's dissolved. Repeat process with salt. To hold the solution use any amply sized wooden receptacle, filling it three-quarters full. Place rolls in this, letting them remain about three weeks, turning them end for end when half the time has elapsed. Then take them out and put in a sunny, airy place where they'll dry thoroughly. Store in a dry place. The bluestone and salt will throw off bluish and yellow flames.

For varied color effects, use the following chemicals added to one gallon of water: For green, use one pound boric acid; for blue, use one pound copper sulfate; for yellow, use one pound ordinary table salt; for purple, one pound potassium permanganate. Soak material in the chemical solution for two minutes. Then remove and dry on old newspapers in a warm room. The same chemicals may be put into holes bored into fireplace logs, then capped with a wooden plug or cork.

Hope you find as much pleasure in these colorful logs as we HAVE. November 13, 1977

Deck The Mantel

It's not what you have, but what you do with it, that gives your house that jolly holiday look. Drape that old narrow market basket, fill it full of bright red apples or Christmas balls, and put it on the mantel. Complete the picture with green boughs, tall red candles and gay stockings awaiting

SANTA. December 15, 1945

Prairie Snowman

An outside Christmas decoration I've made might be helpful to others looking for the unusual. Use three large tumbleweeds to form a snowman, using pipe cleaners to secure them together. Spray with white paint. Heat lamps or light bulbs painted black make the buttons; red and blue tree ornaments the eyes and nose. Add a pipe, old hat, red scarf and earmuffs, and give him a

BROOM. December 5, 1972

Sagebrush Wreaths

One time one of my friends on the treeless plains attended a Wyoming city demonstration given on Christmas decorations.

There were wreaths being made of pine, cedar, juniper and fir at this meeting, but this lady lived 50 miles from evergreens. She wondered what she could use, since she had no decorating material.

In answer to that a wreath was made of sagebrush, applying it in the same way as the evergreens to a wire foundation shaped into a circle. For decoration, wild sunflower-seed pods and other seeds were tinted and inserted into the wreath. A gray-blue bow completed it, and the wreath was just as attractive as those made of evergreens. Besides being something entirely new, it had the added charm of the spicy sage fragrance!

One of the women decided she would make sage wreaths for all her Eastern guests for the holidays.

SAGE. December 21, 1946

Christmas Table Toppers

A festive table always assures a cheery meal. Make snowballs and place them in a mound on a flat plate in the center of the table. Between the snowballs place sprigs of holly or other greens and on the top a bow of red-and-silver ribbon. Holly, mistletoe or evergreens may be placed about the plate. Red, green or silver candles may be used. Recipe for snowballs: Melt 12 marshmallows in ¼ cup milk over hot water. Add ⅓ cup confectioner's sugar and ½ teaspoon vanilla. Beat until smooth. Then take uncooked marshmallows and dip into the mixture, one at a time. Be sure to dip on all sides, then roll them in shredded coconut. This makes 12 snowballs. If you wish to use a little more color in the decorations, you might color the sauce red.

GLADYS ANDERSON. December 22, 1934

Mini-Tree Favors

If you are looking for an idea for Christmas table favors, pine cones make pretty miniature trees. Insert tiny Christmas balls between the scales. Glue on "trunks" made of narrow bottle

CAPS. November 13, 1977

Year 'Round Porch Boxes

Do you have some empty window boxes staring at you as you look out the window? No need to remove them, just turn them into evergreen window boxes. Plant them now, then move them into the garden in the spring. Of course, you must keep them watered so the roots won't dry out. Select the kind of evergreen that is adapted to your climate. A Norway spruce planted in a porch vase is just the thing for an outdoor Christmas tree when Christmas rolls along. Out here in Kansas we have the pretty green cedars that can so easily be transplanted from the hillsides into the porch boxes. Once you start you will do this every year.

EVERGREEN. December 17, 1938

Apple Candle Holders

It's an attractive Christmas centerpiece! It can be yours! Just select five or six large red apples and remove cores, making a cavity in each apple in which to fit small red Christmas candles. Now the apple is a candle holder. Cut a slice off the bottoms so apples stand straight. Then line up the candle-filled apples in the center of the table and surround them with holly or

EVERGREENS. December 22, 1945

Edible Tree Trimming

Why not make edible Christmas tree decorations this year for a change? Wrap popcorn balls in all colors of cellophane. Make Santa faces with big red apples and a bit of cotton. Hang animal cookies and gobs of gumdrops from the branches, and don't forget yards and yards of popcorn on strings.

THE CHILDREN. December 13, 1941

Christmas Star Windows

When everyone on your street or along your road is dressing up the house and lawn for the Christmas festival, try this scene. Trace stars of different sizes on heavy midnight blue paper, placing them not too close together. Cut out the stars, and place blue cellophane over the holes. Glue the blue paper to your windowpanes. When the house is aglow within, the effect will be beautiful.

MRS. W.A.B. December 17, 1932

Scented Trivet

Give you kitchen a wonderful holiday aroma by sewing two potholders together on three sides to create an envelope. Loosely stuff the envelope with pine- or cinnamon-scented potpourri and sew the fourth side together. Use as a trivet. When a hot pot is placed on them the scent is

RELEASED. December 18, 1990

Holds Wreath

Attach an angle iron or shelf bracket near an outside door at about eye level. In the summer, welcome visitors with a colorful pot of flowers hanging from the sturdy holder. In winter, you will have a holder ready for your Christmas

WREATH. December 18, 1990

Basket Will Hold Gifts

This is for grandmas who can't or don't feel able to put up a Christmas tree. If you want someplace to put gifts for the kids, take an old-fashioned bushel basket and paint or decorate the sides with wrapping paper. Put shellac on it, and tie big red or green bows on the handles. This looks festive and holds many

GIFTS. December 4, 1984

Wreaths Still Popular Christmas Decoration

Della Robbia wreaths that originated in the early 1400s are still a popular and appropriate decoration for the holiday season.

Luca della Robbia was a member of a family of artists who lived in Italy about 500 years ago. Working as a goldsmith in his youth, he grew up to become a world-famous sculptor. He is known for his figures of angels and dancing children that he designed upon an elaborate bronze door of a Florence cathedral. After his death in 1495, a nephew, Andrea, and his four sons continued the family tradition. They were famous for their garlands of fruit, flowers, birds and ribbons.Today, della Robbia garlands at Christmas time are still fashionable and can be used in a variety of ways. Evergreen branches, wired to lengths of rope, make garlands that can decorate the mantel, encircle a mirror or entwine a stairway.

To make a wreath, use a base of pine-tree cuttings, a circle of Styrofoam or a moss-covered frame. An assortment of real or artificial fruits and vegetables can be wired to a wreath of pine boughs. For Styrofoam, simple push sprays of greenery around the inside and outside of the circle.

Using plastic fruit, berries can be attached with an ordinary hairpin. Puncture larger fruit with an ice pick. Florist's wire with a bit of glue on one end can be pushed into the fruit, the other end into the base. A slight dent or "nest" can be made in the Styrofoam with a hammer so the fruit will fit snugly. Fill empty spaces with additional greens, nuts or berries, giving the wreath a bountiful appearance.

For a party, fresh fruit—such as lemons, oranges, grapefruit and limes—can be wired to a garland of artificial greens and arranged around a doorway. Tack gold ribbons and bows to corners.

For a truly different Christmas, fashion a wreath of various evergreens. Attach cobs of corn for the cardinals, hang clusters of small mesh bags filled with tiny acorns for the blue jays, suet rolled bird seed and several "faces" of the sunflower. Replace traditional bows with a cluster of large red apples. Hang this lush wreath against the barn or house and
ENJOY! November 25, 1978

Cartons Are Handy

Save those oatmeal cartons. They make wonderful containers for gift-giving when filled with home-canned fruit, pickles or preserves. Wrap them prettily and add a ribbon for an attractive and thoughtful
GIFT. December 8, 1981

Merry Mailbox

For many years we have decorated our rural mailbox with evergreens, pine cones, plastic outdoor ribbons and a Christmas greeting that is tall enough to be read from the highway.

Two years ago we had the house painted at a cost of several hundred dollars. But we had more compliments from the holiday mailbox that cost less than a dollar! Aren't people
FUNNY? December 28, 1967

Guests Can Eat The Cookie Tree

Make a Christmas cookie tree for a different kind of decoration, then share it with the family when you dismantle it.

You will need the following ingredients:

9 cups	sifted all-purpose flour
9 tsp	baking powder
4½ tsp	ginger
1½ tsp	salt
1 cup	butter or margarine
1 cup	brown sugar, firmly packed
2 cups	molasses
3 eggs	

Red and silver candies

Large green gumdrops

Measure flour, baking powder, ginger and salt and sift together. Cream butter until soft and fluffy. Add brown sugar gradually, creaming well. Beat in molasses and eggs. Add dry ingredients and blend well.

Cover bowl and chill dough until firm enough to roll with a rolling pin. Roll dough a quarter-inch thick. Make cardboard patterns of stars in graduated sizes. Using patterns on dough, cut out stars. Cut a small hole in the center of each star. Bake in a preheated 350 degree oven for eight minutes. Remove immediately to wire rack to cool.

To assemble tree, decorate stars with green frosting and trim edges with red and silver candies, pressing into frosting while soft. Place largest star on a knitting needle or similar object. Add a gumdrop next. Then the next largest cookie is threaded onto the needle, then a gumdrop. Continue, separating cookies with gumdrops.

If desired, top the tree with two cookie angels. This would make an unusual and lovely centerpiece for a Christmas party. Guests could take cookies home as

FAVORS. December 12, 1978

Decorates Yard

My husband came up with a wonderful Christmas decoration. He made lamps out of bleach bottles by cutting a letter in each bottle to spell out "Merry Christmas." Then he put a small Christmas light in each bottle. It decorated our yard and was simply
                    BEAUTIFUL. December 17-24, 1963

Timeless Traditions

Chapter 6

*F*AMILY TRADITIONS ARE as unique as the ancestors and ethnic backgrounds that inspire them, but all share a common bond—the ability to tie generations and family celebrations together year after year.

My readers have shared dozens of their traditions for making Christmas a special time, many of which are included on the following pages. Some are simple phrases and poems recited every Christmas. Others center around Bible readings that celebrate Jesus' birth. As you read about these traditions—some entertaining, some poignant—you will no doubt remember many priceless traditions of your own.

Christmas At Grandma's

Almost every Christmas story seems to take it for granted that grandmother lived in the country and all the family went there to spend Christmas. It was completely reversed in our case, because we lived in the country and went to the city for Christmas.

The bright lights and city noises lent enchantment to the wonderful event, as did mysterious goings-on behind the closed doors of the parlor.

Grandmother had a large house, but it was taxed to capacity with aunts, uncles and cousins. Beds were at a premium, and cots were set up almost anywhere in the house. I remember how we used to lie in our cots tucked up under the eaves, trying in vain to stay awake long enough to hear Santa and his reindeer, but we never quite made it.

In the morning the parlor doors were opened, and we could see the great tree with presents for everyone. I think Grandmother must have worked for weeks to get ready for this day, and everything was perfection.

I was still a child when Grandmother left us. Since we are scattered to the four corners of the country, family gatherings have become a thing of the past. But she left such a beautiful memory I cannot think of Christmas without remembering the priceless happiness she gave us. Truly, she endowed us with the Christmas spirit.

OLD TIMER. December 23, 1944

Are The Lights On The Tree?

I am 55 years old, and have been night supervisor at the Oklahoma Children's Memorial Hospital for the past 21 years. Santa visits our children with gifts on Christmas morning, and carolers follow. Some of these people have been coming for 15 years.

I still carry on a tradition in my family. My parents are both dead and I am an only child. In 1938, we got our first electricity in a small town named Cooperton in southwest Oklahoma. We added a rock living room to our house. Just outside the room was a little cedar tree that stuck up about five inches above the picket fence.

My parents bought an electric star and a string of 25 lights for the tree. We were so excited about lighting the tree.

The tree is now 28 feet tall. There are 387 lights plus the original star. For 13 years no one has lived in the house. I drive the 130 miles there the first week in December. A neighbor helps me put up the lights. They are on a timer and go off and on automatically. I take the lights down over New Year's.

There are only 24 people living in this town now. I go there every three or four weeks all though the year and plan to move back when I retire.

If I could do only one thing at Christmas, it would be putting the lights on the tree. In many of my Christmas cards, they ask, "Are the lights on the tree?" Most add, "I'll bet they are." They have been put up in all kinds of weather: rain, snow and sunshine. Years bring changes, but the way I celebrate Christmas will never
CHANGE. December 11, 1979

Treasures Tradition

Even in this day when we "have it so good," we need not leave out the special things in life. I think it's up to us to make life meaningful.

At Christmas our family has a tradition that means much to me; I look forward to it just as much, if not more, as anything else at Christmas time. On Christmas Eve we all gather in the living room. My dad gets the Bible and reads the two accounts of the birth of Jesus. Then we all kneel together in a time of family prayer. This time together is so precious that since I've been married, I still try to go home on Christmas Eve.

My parents may not even know what they make Christmas mean by keeping this tradition, but it has made me realize how much more Christmas really means than mere gifts or gay decorations. I'm hoping in some way I can help my two little girls come to feel as I do. Thank you for giving me this opportunity to express the feelings of my
HEART. December 17-24, 1963

One For Each Child

The first Christmas we had a grandchild, I started an ornament collection for him. Now, as each grandchild joins our family we add an ornament. I try to buy unbreakable ones, and Grandpa, with his etching pen, prints the child's name and year on it (a tiny glued-on label could serve this purpose).

We hang the ornaments on our tree, and on Christmas Day each child gets to remove his and take it home with him. By the time our grandchildren are married they'll have a nice collection of ornaments for their own tree and, we hope, fond memories of the Grandpa and Grandma who gave

THEM. December 28, 1978

Stockings Were Hung On A Chair

I don't suppose most people have been fortunate enough to have had a "chair Christmas." It was a custom handed down from my grandmother.

Grandmother Lurana E. Taylor homesteaded on the Nebraska prairies. There was no wood to build a house, so they lived in a sod house. When Christmas came around, there were no fireplaces or Christmas trees. So, as most of the western pioneers did, she used a kitchen chair to anchor the stockings. Santa wasn't a bit bashful about leaving gifts in stockings, even if they were pinned to the back of a chair.

One of the gifts Mother found in her stocking and kept for years was a hand-carved jumping jack her brother made.

The first Christmas I can remember, my older brother and I celebrated on a farm in Wisconsin. At this time some homes had Christmas trees with candles for lights. They were expensive and apt to go up in a puff of smoke. Needless to say, we didn't have a tree.

Mother got us ready for bed on Christmas Eve, rubbing us good with warm skunk oil (it didn't smell) and putting on our warm sleepers. Afterward our long black stockings (my brother wore them over his long underwear the same as I did) were pinned on a chair. Mother then carried the kerosene lamp and took us upstairs. We crawled into our cold beds and pulled the patchwork quilts over our heads. Mother went downstairs. We settled down to listen for the reindeer hooves scraping on the roof and dropped off to sleep.

Christmas morning we were up before daylight. Mother lit the lamp, and Dad stocked chunks into the round-oak heating stove. Our stockings bulged with candy, nuts, and an orange in the toe. It was the only orange we ever had and it was prized. On the chair seat was a doll for me. It was plain, with a painted face and hair, but to me it was beautiful. I enjoyed hours of play with it. My brother got a marble game called Handy Andy. Once he got a tin can, and when he rolled it away from him it came back. It quite mystified us.

In Wisconsin, we had our first Christmas tree. Now everyone has a tree, and the gifts are limited only by one's pocketbook. But nothing can be quite as satisfying to me as my "chair Christmas" of long

AGO. December 13, 1977

Baked Cake For Jesus' Birthday

I am a firm believer in Santa Claus. But to insure the true meaning of Christmas Day when the children were young, I baked a big fruit cake early in December. Later, the cake was iced with yellow frosting and orange-tinted coconut to resemble straw.

In the center of the cake I placed a small plastic crèche surrounded by 10 to 14 candles. Each evening, when the children were home from school, they took turns lighting one new candle and re-lighting the ones from previous nights. Then each had a small piece of cake.

Before lighting the nightly candle the chosen child made a prayer or a good wish for Jesus. On Christmas Eve the last candle and all the others were relit while singing Happy Birthday to Jesus.

Now in their teens, the young folks still ask me to bake the Jesus Cake. It has become a

TRADITION. December 2, 1975

Quilt Is A Tradition

Like most families, we have many Christmas traditions, but the one that stands out in my mind began in a surprising way. Since the floors in our house were always cold, each Christmas morning I would spread a quilt on the floor in front of the wood stove for the children to sit on while opening their stockings.

When our first grandchild was 1 year old, I was visiting in his home at Christmas time. My daughter carefully spread a quilt on the floor for him to sit on while seeing what Santa had brought. I asked her why she did that when she had a furnace and carpeted floors. She replied, "Why, Mother, it wouldn't be Christmas without sitting on a

QUILT." December 26, 1978

Being Home At Christmas

Most people want to be home for Christmas. Some, like myself, will travel great distances to be there for Christmas Eve. It is at Christmas, more than any other time of the year, that we remember the home where we grew up. And so, I look forward to this special time.

Once home, it's fun to see Grandpa put up the tree he chopped down himself... to hear Grandma say, "I told you it would be too big for the living room. It's a church tree." They have been arguing pro and con like that for as long as I can remember. My sister will come hurrying into the house, showing off small Ann in her angel costume on their way to the Christmas play.

The small fry visiting Grandma will check up on the difference between Santa's girth and the width of the fireplace. He'll surely get down, but he'll be all black with soot. Through it all, there will be a pervading feeling of merriment, bustle and cheer. Then, adding a touch of reverence, will come the lyric notes of "O Come, All Ye Faithful," pealing softly from the church on the square that I attended so many years before I left home.

The words of Edgar Guest's poem, "Are You Going Home for Christmas" come to my mind each year as we go winging through the skies. His words: "Are you going home for Christmas? Have you written you'll be there; going home to greet the mother and to show her that you care. Going home to greet the father in a way to make him glad—if you're not, I hope there'll never come a time you'll wish you had..."

Comes Christmas Day and church services, carols, the sight of relatives and old friends, the cheery greetings, the huge get-together around the dinner table, reminiscing of other days gone by—then, the lighting of the tree. All too soon the day comes to an end. Going home again is what I really like best about the
HOLIDAYS. December 15, 1970

North Woods Christmas Custom

Many years ago, when I was a teenager, we lived in heavily wooded northern Wisconsin, where there were people of many nationalities. Most of them were without many of this world's goods, but all of them were wonderful friends.

The nicest part of the holiday season came when the first hob-goblins and such appeared at our door after dark on Christmas evening. They burst in the door the minute it was cracked open. Although it nearly scared me witless the first time, I learned to look forward to the wild melee after that. All the people were masked and dressed in old clothes; the idea was to guess their identities.

My parents thoroughly enjoyed the guessing. After it was over they all visited awhile, gathered a few more—especially the young people—as they went along, and had refreshments if any were available. Sometimes there would be a long distance to walk, but it was used in singing, and it certainly was a nice way to spend the time.

My father said it was a custom in his native Virginia, but it was a family of Swiss descent that started it in our Wisconsin area. It didn't cost much money, but we could really look forward to it. I am sure we enjoyed this as much as the young do their gifts and presents of today, and I expect it left a more lasting
IMPRESSION. December 16-23, 1969

Christmas Is A Lighted Candle

My husband frowns on lighted candles. He thinks they are a fire hazard. So for 11 months of the year I go along with him.

But on the first of December out come my candles, for Christmas to me is a lighted candle. We make our own and, as a safety precaution, we make wide-based ones that aren't apt to tip over. We put them in every type of container—cups, glasses and old Avon jars (which, incidentally, give off a pleasant scent).

I love to write our Christmas cards with a candle flickering dreamily nearby. I keep one lit in a container in the bathroom. The fragrance it gives off drifts into the hall and bedrooms, making the whole house smell Christmasy.

I've already dug out our candle-making supplies. Soon the "kids" and I will start on my favorite chore, making our December supply of

CANDLES. November 30, 1976

Turkey Song Continues

In the October issue of "Heart of the Home," the subject of traditions concerning Thanksgiving and Christmas made me think of a song my husband's father used to sing whenever turkey was served and our family would gather around for the feast.

Invariably, someone would ask "Pop" to sing the "Turkey Song," which originated with him.

Here is the song, which was sung to the tune of "America":

My turkey, 'tis of thee,
Sweet bird of cranberry, of thee I sing.
I love thy thigh and wing,
Leg, back and everything.
My mouth goes ting-a-ling with thoughts of thee.

Pop has been gone now for nearly 20 years, but his children and grandchildren still sing this song whenever Thanksgiving or Christmas turkey is

SERVED! December 21, 1993

72

Christmas Is For Children Of All Ages

What do I like best about Christmas? I'm a married woman of 29, and mother of four, but I'm still a child at heart when it comes to Christmas. Our three oldest know all about who pays the bills, but they still believe in Santa Claus, and they know that their mother does, too!

Christmas is for the children, and the best part of Christmas is just watching them enjoy it. I love to see their faces when they see the towns lighted with all the Christmas decorations, and when they are in front of a Sunday School audience telling the age-old story of the babe in the manger. I love the family dinners when all the cousins are there and you can eat as much dinner, dessert and Christmas candy as you want to, and the wee ones who are seeing a Christmas tree or department store Santa for the first time. How their faces light up! And then, of course, my favorite is seeing their faces on Christmas morning. "Santa really did leave something— just for me," they seem to say.

The best part of Christmas is the children. It all started with a baby in a manger. We should always keep the faith and love in Christmas for the

CHILDREN. November 30, 1971

They Miss Christmas In Snow

This time of year, some folks, who have been reared in the Midwest and transplanted to a year-round warm climate, suffer a familiar, dull ache for Christmas in the snow. For among their fondest memories of early years are those of knee-high boots in crusty snow, red-tipped ears and frosty noses, the warmth of a crackling fire, and the unexplainable glamour of a clear, crisp, star-studded sky. To me, this is Christmas!

The Far West was an abrupt change for our family. Temperatures are often mild on Christmas night, and doors are left ajar to let in the cool, fresh evening air. Garden chrysanthemums bloom profusely, and friends remember us annually with a generous bouquet on this holy night. And if, by merry chance, the day is somewhat overcast or blessed with a drizzlelike rain, the family is delighted! "Just like home!" they remark with glee.

But why should this be so? Why do we yearn for snow on Christmas, when the blessed Holy Land had none? What more fitting place than our desert, so similar to the sight of Christ's birth! Did He not live in a wilderness of warm sun, golden sand and rustling palms, and walk along dusty trails among desert plants, so very much like ours in the Southwest?

We should, by all reason, feel especially fortunate this holiday season, knowing He followed this similar path; yet in spite of all this there is still something mysteriously enchanting about a Midwest winter, and Christmas

IN THE SNOW! December 7, 1971

Season Takes Me Home

The snow may be just as white when it falls here in the city as it is in my mountain village, but it lacks an ethereal quality that I cannot define.

The people here in the city may be just as good as those in my home village, but friendliness and loyalty are characteristic among my village friends, while I have failed to find them here.

The streets and stores here in the city are beautifully decorated for Christmas, but I prefer the appearance of my village, surrounded by the wooded mountains where I may walk a little way from our door and be among the living Christmas trees—pines, spruces, firs and cedars—with their sweet perfumes and the wind making music in their branches.

Oh, yes, I'm going home for Christmas!

SYLVIA. December 21, 1946

"O Holy Night" Duet Continues

My younger sister and I have an unusual Christmas tradition that we have kept for many years and hope to keep for many more. It all started when we were quite young. "O Holy Night" happened to be our favorite Christmas song, and we would faithfully sing it every Christmas Eve. Neither of us could carry a tune then, nor can we now, so the rest of the family thought it was funny. It was very touching to us, so we let them laugh and kept on singing.

As we grew older, we were not together at Christmas time. A phone call from her on our first Christmas apart found us tearful, sad and missing each other. I told her how much I was going to miss our "O Holy Night" duo. She replied, "Well, let's sing it now."

There we were, on long distance, singing our favorite song. Needless to say, we were laughing and happy when we hung up.

Every year we make our call and sing to our hearts' content. My children and husband think I'm crazy, but they'll never know how much that call fulfills my
CHRISTMAS! December 9, 1980

Black Cats Exchanged

About 1930 or '31, when we were all still at home, we tried something new for Christmas. With eight in the family, we decided to exchange names, as well as giving each other gifts as usual. We had to make something for that person. I drew my sister's name and made her a stuffed black cat about five or six inches high.

That cat is still in existence, and many, many more have appeared since. The original cat has been recovered with gray material and awarded a 50th medal. It was once caught by a rat, killed, and put in a coffin, but as cats have nine lives, it reappears occasionally.

My sister and I are the main ones giving black cats to each other, but others have taken part. I have quite a collection now and so has she. Some are bought, many are homemade; they all have various uses.

Each Christmas, we look for mysterious-looking packages containing a black cat with a note or poem. We've had a great time continuing this tradition for 50
YEARS. December 6, 1988

Stir Holiday "Pudding" With Laughter

The Christmas Pudding has been in my cookbook since 1935. It was given to me by an old gentleman from Lindsborg, Kansas.

He stayed with my parents for several days and would do odd jobs for his board and room. He always slept in the barn loft. His destination was North Dakota. My father usually took him to his next stop, which was with a Swedish family. He would walk about 15 miles a day, and on his return home, he followed the same pattern.

The Christmas Pudding

Take some human nature as you find
The commonest variety will do—
Put a little graciousness behind it
Add a lump of charity or two
Squeeze in just a drop of moderation,
Half as much frugality or less
Add some very fine consideration,
Strain off all of poverty's distress
Pour some milk of human kindness in
Stir it up with laughter every minute
Season with good will toward man.
Leave it till the jolly bubbles rise,
Sprinkle it with kisses for confection
Flavor it with the children's merry chatter
Frost it with the snow of wintry dells
Place it on a holly-garnished platter
And serve it with the song of Christmas bells.

—Author unknown

The Christmas Pudding has been an inspiration to me through the years as well as at

CHRISTMAS. December 16-23, 1969

Try To Say "Christmas Gift" First

The tradition in our family is to be the first to say "Christmas gift." My parents did this as far back as I can remember. Either Mom or Dad would go quietly downstairs and get a nice warm fire going in the wood heating stove, then open the stairway door and call to my two brothers and me, "Christmas gift."

We usually dressed by the warm "drum" around the stove-pipe, which came through the floor to the bedroom. However, when we heard "Christmas gift," we hurriedly grabbed our clothes and dashed down to see what Santa Claus had brought.

My brothers and I have continued this with our children. Now, even though we live far apart, each Christmas morning we put in a phone call to say "Christmas gift" to each

OTHER. December 17, 1985

The Lookout Man

Our family Christmas tradition was observed every year while we were youngsters. We lived on a farm in eastern Kansas. We had a lovely apple orchard and every fall buried apples for winter use.

About two weeks before Christmas we were always visited by "The Lookout Man." This was Santa's helper, and he was attired exactly like Santa. He would suddenly appear at our large window, tap on it, and thus check up on our behavior to report back to Santa. My, how he could improve our behavior! I was the world's slowest in undressing, but the minute he appeared, I made record time getting into my nightie. Our cousin was an ardent thumb sucker, but that thumb would come out of her mouth at once when The Lookout Man appeared. We were always at our best for him. You may wonder how the apple orchard was connected with all this. As youngsters, we didn't get the connection, but in later years it dawned on us that The Lookout Man always showed up on the evenings our dad went out to the orchard for apples.

No more do we have The Lookout Man, but our family ties are close, and he is always mentioned. Many memories are revived on Christmas when we gather at our oldest sister's home for noonday Christmas dinner. We still have The Lookout Man with us in our beloved dad, and all of us are thankful

FOR THAT. December 18, 1956

Children Perform First

My husband's family has a Christmas tradition that I think is pretty unique. When he and his brothers and sisters were little, they came up with the idea of putting on plays and skits for their parents before they opened their presents on Christmas Eve. (Maybe they were threatened that they wouldn't get to open presents if they didn't perform.)

The skits were certainly not impromptu. The older children organized everything, and rehearsals were held secretly. My husband has fond memories of the fun.

Now the extended family gathers together on Christmas Eve, and the original performers' children are asked to perform. They are threatened with no gifts if they don't. No skits or plays are put on, but we usually get serenaded and told jokes. Even though some of the kids are somewhat reluctant, their antics are fondly remembered year

AFTER YEAR. December 9, 1986

Christmas Morning

We have a large family, and every year, in spite of good intentions, we find ourselves on Christmas Eve with the children's gifts still unwrapped. We hide them all in big, brown boxes and promise each other that next year we'll get them all wrapped in pretty packages.

Yesterday, our 9-year-old had to write a composition on "What We Always Do on Christmas." She wrote: "Early in the morning, Daddy puts on the big record, the one that's always just organ music and chimes and you hear it even before you are awake. We open our stockings and the packages from relatives first, and all the time we keep looking, 'til it seems we simply can't wait, at the BIG BROWN BOXES that hold the things we want the most."

Suddenly, I realized that we'd established a Christmas tradition dear to the hearts of the children. They may not be glamorous, but in the years to come, around our tree you'll find the beloved, exciting

BIG BROWN BOXES. December 23, 1958

Liberated Nazi Flag Becomes Tree Skirt

During World War II, my husband was involved in the infamous Battle of the Bulge, which took place in December. Christmas was very lonely for both of us and made even more stressful for me because of the news blackout.

During that engagement, my mate liberated a large German flag of red material with a swastika appliquéd in the center. When peace was declared he came home, bringing the flag.

The next Christmas I removed the swastika and made a Christmas tree skirt of the bright red cotton material.

The flag has been used every year since. With the removal of the swastika—symbol of hatred and war—the flag has been converted into a useful part of celebrating the birth of Christ, who came to change our lives and bring

PEACE! December 17, 1985

Hang Up Your Stockings

Everyone hangs up a Christmas stocking at our house! They are all the same size, made of red felt with a white band across the top. The name of the owner is embroidered in dark green thread.

The idea started when we adults and the older children watched enviously as the little ones explored their bulging stockings. At first, we were afraid there would not be enough small gifts to make any sort of showing. They had to be inexpensive. We soon learned that there are an amazing number of appreciated small gifts that can be purchased for a nominal sum.

For the little ones there are the tiny toys: dolls, puzzles, cars, planes, crayons and paint boxes. For the older folks there are inexpensive handkerchiefs, small bottles of cologne, books of stamps, pieces of costume jewelry, art gum erasers, pencils, even toothbrushes with gay-colored handles. For the masculine members of the family it's fun to buy pen knives, key rings, a couple of cigars of a special brand, shaving creams and lotions or shoe polish. Our camera enthusiast receives rolls of film and darkroom supplies; our fisherman gets trout flies and other gear; our stamp collector is pleased with packets of stamps and stamp hinges.

On Christmas Eve the stockings go up. From the many secret corners of the house come the small packages. By the time the children are ready for bed, the stockings are bulging. Last year we added another stocking. This one is for the house. It was fun for the whole family to explore it. There was a window washer, a set of colorful measuring spoons, small boxes of matches, a set of coasters and a box of chalk for the bulletin board.

Why not have a Christmas stocking for each member of the family? We're never too old to enjoy the fun, and it's such a pleasant CHRISTMAS CUSTOM. December 20, 1955

Time To Set Up Christmas Shelf

When Thanksgiving is over we get our Christmas reading together. We have a special shelf set aside for just these books.

What books? The Bible, of course, with the Nativity story; Dickens' *Christmas Carol* and *The Bird's Christmas Carol*; and, we must read again about the March family in *Little Women* giving away their Christmas morning breakfast.

There are other books, all about Christmas, many for the little folks whose eyes grow brighter each day as we wait for the man in the red suit to come. How do they celebrate Christmas in other countries? We have a book on Christmas customs, and as we plan for our American Christmas, it is fun to read about what others do around the world.

Then there is the Christmas Scrapbook. Here stories, legends and bits of verse are clipped from papers and magazines. More is added to it each year.

When read-aloud time comes after dinner, books are chosen from this shelf. We read them last year and we'll read them again next year. The Christmas spirit and season seem to bring new life and interest to the old stories.

Another special book on the shelf is the Christmas Diary. Each year we put little mementos into it—the Christmas napkin, the church program, party invitations, the letter from a friend whom we hadn't heard from for a long time, the "Oh, so beautiful!" Christmas card. Then everyone writes a little Christmas note that includes what it meant to them and which gift, what incident, had special significance.

Now I must add one more item to my shopping list. Another copy of *The Night Before Christmas*. The old one is virtually in tatters, and without that book it just wouldn't be our Christmas

SHELF. December 17-24, 1968

Grandpa's Grab Bag

Grandpa's contribution to Christmas Day festivities consists of a grab bag for the children. Small toys, packages of Life Savers, pencil tablets—many things costing no more than a dime have been accumulated and wrapped separately. I suspect Grandma helps with this during the year.

After noontime, when toys from the tree have all been examined, the children gather 'round for the excitement of pulling surprises from Grandpa's pack. There are enough surprises for several turns, and each must unwrap and show his gift before the next one draws. Hilarity rivals that of the early morning, and the ceremony is followed by a session of trading hair ribbons for packages of tacks or bobby pins for

LOLLIPOPS. December 23, 1958

CHRISTMAS WITH KATE

Christmas Verses

Chapter 7

THE SIGHTS AND sounds of Christmas have inspired countless readers to put their pens to paper and wax poetically about their favorite part of the holidays. Their beautiful verses capture images as diverse as the tranquility of snowy Christmas mornings and the angelic behavior of children who know that Santa Claus is watching. All of them are sure to get you into the holiday spirit.

Let these poetic tributes to the season inspire you. After reading them, you may just want to write some verses of your own.

Swan Lake Christmas

December snow fell deep in that far country.
There were no evergreens; the road to town
Some 15 miles away soon drifted shut.
Ma made a Christmas tree from an oak sapling,
Hung it with popcorn, cranberries, paper bells.
But still the youngest children worried, asked
Could Santa find them in this wilderness?
Ma and the older sisters worked with wool.
While in the barn Pa fashioned wooden toys —
And Christmas morning Santa found the way;
The children woke to hear him right outside!
(Pa, shaking harness bells, had raced around the house.)

Elizabeth Shafer, December 16-23, 1975

"If" For Christmas

If you can keep the right perspective,
Remembering the meaning of the day,
If you can see commercialism rampant,
Yet in your own life let it not hold sway;
If you can see beyond the brazen beauty
Of ornaments, pretense and street display;
If you can think in terms of love, not money,
And see a Star, forgetting Santa and his sleigh;

If you can walk through crowds and be unruffled,
Or work with those whose tempers tire and fray,
If neither noise nor discord can disturb you,
If, in confusion, you take time to pray;
If you can demonstrate the joy of Christmas,
(Within your own heart let the Babe be born)
If you can share your joy in song and service—
How wonderful will be your Christmas morn.

Rae Cross, December 5, 1972

84

And Christmas Was

There was a tree
With shiny tinsel
but Christmas wasn't.
There were some lights
In many colors
but Christmas wasn't.
There were some gifts
And there were cards
There was hurry
And the crowds
but Christmas wasn't.
Then, at last, there was love—
And Christmas was.

Beryl Frank, December 17-24, 1974

Christmas Music

From great cathedrals' organ lofts,
From wayside chapel choirs,
From churches of divergent creeds,
One blended theme inspires
The world to sing at Christmas time
United to proclaim
The angels' song of joy and peace,
Revere the Savior's name.

The singing hearts are close to God
As harmonizing strains
Revive the spirit, fill the soul
With comfort that remains
Through daily tasks that call for grace
When cares and trials press;
The old loved carols echoing
Sustain and cheer and bless.

Delia Adams Leitner, December 25, 1956

When Christmas Comes
Have you any old grudge you would like to pay
Any wrong laid up from a bygone day?
Gather them now and lay them away
When Christmas comes.

Hard thoughts are heavy to carry, my friend
And life is short from beginning to end;
Be kind to yourself, leave nothing to mend
When Christmas comes.

William Lytle, December 13, 1941

Yes, Virginia, There Is A Santa Claus
The very idea of a big 8-year-old girl like you
Letting your little playmates kid you
Into wondering if there really is a Santa Claus.
It was all right for your mother or grandmother
'Way back in '97 to write to the *New York Sun*,
And getting a world-famous editorial in reply.
Because in those distant days
It was the custom to shush little girls
When they asked too many questions;
They weren't supposed to know much.
That was 35 years ago—Tempus fugit;
But what is more to the point:
"Tempora mutantur, et nos mutamur in illis"—
Which, according to the dictionary, means
The times are changed, and we are changed with them;
Particularly little 8-year-old girls
Who in those times at that age
Know more than their grandmothers ever knew.

Yes, Virginia, there is a Santa Claus—
A big, roly-poly, pink-cheeked fellow
With bushy whiskers and red pants 'n' everything.

But, Virginia dear, you've heard, of course
That there has been and still is a depression
Which all of us have felt more or less.
Even our beloved St. Nicholas,
Which is another name for Kris Kringle,
Has had to take a cut—and it's tough
Slicing steaks from reindeer.
But he hasn't quit; he's still carrying on;
And, even though he may not have so many reindeer,
And his pack may not be quite so full this year,
And the jingle bells not quite so loud as before,
Don't forget this important point, Virginia,
That Santy, himself, is a whole lot thinner
And we're sure he'll be able this Christmas
To squeeze down a lot of small chimneys
That he just couldn't get through in days gone by.
Yes, indeed, Virginia, there is a Santa Claus;
There always has been and there always will be.

L.R. Booth, December 24, 1932

Birthday For A Boy

I like to think of Jesus
As a laughing, running boy,
Coming home with rosy cheeks,
Eyes shining, full of joy.
I like to think that Joseph
Had carved a special toy,
And Mary made a sweetened cake,
With love for a small boy.
I like to think that Christmas
Was to them, just as today,
A loving celebration
For a "Happy Birthday."

Helen Scott Wylie, December 1-8, 1964

Just Before Christmas

The kiddies are like angels, they are so very good.
Sister washes up the dishes while Brother carries wood.
They do their humble daily tasks so quick and willingly,
I stop and wonder at the cause, something's changed them, I can see.
They ask me if there's more to do, and they don't complain at all,
Then Sister slyly mentions dolls, and Brother says, "What a swell football."
At last, I clearly see the reason my kids have been so dear.
It's the magic of the season and Christmas Day is almost here.

Ellen Cosens, December 17, 1938

Spell Christmas

Some of the best things in life spell C-H-R-I-S-T-M-A-S:
Children, with their eager enthusiasm.
Home, with its heartening welcome.
Religion, with its spiritual solace.
Idealism, with its belief in goodness.
Sentiment, with its lasting memories.
Thoughtfulness, with its friendly cheer.
Merriment, with its sparkling gladness.
Affection, with its tender devotion.
Selflessness, with its rewarding satisfaction.
Yes, many of the best things in life spell Christmas!

Arizona, December 22, 1945

It's December!

December is: Silvery, sharp stars and the crunch of snow. Counting pennies. Secrets. School windows with fat Santa Clauses and bells and a babe in the manger. A sprig of holly in Grandpa's lapel. The scent of bayberry. Trying to find where you hid those gifts you bought last summer. A candle at dusk. December is Christmas and believing.

Kansas, December 7-14, 1970

Wreath For Door

Let this green wreath testify
to the people passing by
that here resides a cordial one
who has a heart as warm as sun,
loves verdure and the myriad joys
of nuts and food and children's toys
and music. May the ribbons show
that you are gay and good to know
and wish the whole world happiness
and, should they call, your smile would bless
them with the cheer of Christmastide
and draw them, like a friend, inside.

Helen Harrington, December 7-14, 1971

Peace To You

Deep peace of the running wave to you
deep peace of the flowing air to you
deep peace of the quiet Earth to you
deep peace of the shining stars to you
deep peace of the Son of Peace to you.

Fiona McLeod, December 26, 1972

On Christmas Night

Heap high the Christmas hearth tonight,
Bid friends to share its glow.
Let there be warmth and food and light,
And laughter's sparkling flow.

But if one enters, hungry, spent,
With spirit sorrow-pressed,
As you give welcome, be content;
The Lord Christ is your guest.

Edith Porteus Thayer, December 20, 1941

Greeting Card
Writing your holiday card,
I remember the laughing light
That filled a room when you were there...
The gentle mischief of the words you said
To make me smile... and all the time,
The wise compassion in your eyes!
I remember striding after you on stars
Down a winter street, window shopping, laughing—
Always the laughter and the sweetness and the warmth
Of loving you.
I seal the envelope, and smile,
Glad with remembering.
                    Lee Avery Reed, December 3-10, 1974

Christmas Thoughts
Was baby Jesus just as pink
And soft and warm and small,
With damp dark curls about His neck
Or just no hair at all?

As new, with eyes as fathomless
As any shadowed lake—
All curled up kitten-wise in sleep
Or starfish when awake?

And did He wave an aimless fist
And start at sudden sound,
And did His small chin quiver...
And when they gathered 'round
Did Mary smile, and half-afraid
To touch the Little One,
Say tenderly, "His Father knew
That He would have a Son."
                    Margaret Hillert, December 19-26, 1961

A Christmas Thought

Christmas time recalls to mind such dear, familiar things
As drifted snow, and Christmas trees, bright lights and
popcorn strings,
Gay greetings, cards and packages, tinsel and angel wings.
There's mistletoe and evergreen, and holly wreath to greet
The host of loved ones come to call, friends passing on the street;
And candies, cake and cookies to make a festive treat.
But while we dream of Christmas, cold and white with snow,
It's Christmas, too, where days are hot and the sun is all aglow,
For Christmas knows no boundaries—it's everywhere you go!
                    Mildred Hoskinson, December 18, 1956

The Mystery

"I'se dot you Trisman present,"
Said my 3-year-old to me,
As she showed me a crumpled package
And waved it gleefully.

"It's square and white and it's dot some lace,
And you blow your nose on it, too.
But don't you guess what it is, 'cause then
I couldn't give it to you."

So I guessed a dress, but it wasn't that
Or an apron maybe? but, oh—
She laughed and crowed and clapped her hands
And the answer she said was "No!"

Yet, I know that on Christmas there'll be no gift
That will make my day a song—
One half so much as this mystery
I'm to blow my nose upon!
                    Mrs. E.D. Stewart, December 18, 1937

Ritual

The good smell of the forest fills the house.
A gay confusion has the heart in thrall,
selecting, choosing what the tree shall wear,
decked like a princess for a festival.
Quaint, sentimental treasures of the past
emerge from wrappings to participate
with garish novelties. We recognize
parts of old patterns in the one we make
anew each year: not perfect, not complete,
but with an ageless Angel set above
the toys and tinsel, at her feet a Star
resplendent with the many lights of love.

R.H. Grenville, December 19, 1972

Which Gift Was Gold?

It is not the weight of jewel or plate
Or the rustle of silk or fur.
But the spirit in which the gift is rich
As the gifts of the Wise Men were.
And we are not told whose gift was gold
or whose was the gift of myrrh.

E.K. Watson, December 20, 1941

Santa Claus

You wonder if there is a Santa Claus,
You've never seen him, you say?
Child, he's been traveling over the world
For two thousand years and a day.
Haven't you found his spinning tops,
His dolls and his round red drums?
Then certain it is that once a year
The King of the Far North comes!

Never you'll see his crimson cloak
As red as a candy cane;
Never you'll hear his reindeer' hooves
Rattle the windowpane.
But when did you see the Man in the Moon,
Or fairies or goblins or elves?
Yet you believe when you read of them
In books on your nursery shelves!

The only things that are real and true
Are fantasy, faith, romance,
And the magic ring by the wishing tree
Where the feet of the pixies dance.
Always there's been a Santa Claus
Since that day in an Eastern land
When the angels sang to a newborn babe—
Child, do you understand?

Helen Weishimer, December 18, 1937

Country Christmas
The country keeps Christmas with silence and snow
and stars in the heavens and cattle below,
with songs in the trees and winds that increase
the feeling of spaciousness, wisdom and peace.

The lamps in the houses cast long beams of light
like highways that welcome you in from the night.
The smoke from the chimneys shelters the farms,
the barns and the houses like loving, warm arms.

Thoughts and the sunsets are sparkling and wide,
time has a reach here, a mind to abide,
drifts, dreams, philosophies, duties run deep—
a Christmas time beauty for country to keep.

Helen Harrington, December 15, 1970

For So Much Christmas

My heart could wish no Christmas
More perfect to remember—
The tree aglow with red
And green and muted amber,
The child's eyes softly eager,
But with no hint of greed,
The husband, who was circling
Wide oceans till December
Now come to anchor here
In love's sweet circle, safe.
Within my heart
A thousand bells ring out
My thanks for Christmas—
For love, and home, and hope;
Not even Handel's "Hallelujah"
Can out-sing my joy!

Doris Kerns Quinn, December 15-22, 1964

Visions Of The Far East

Wrapped in tissue
Dates and figs lumped the red stocking
Draped lovingly
Over white tissue-wrapped presents,
Gifts from my dad
Under my side of the tree.
While tasting those Far East delicacies
I savored every bite
Imagining rubies, emeralds, camels
And drifting sands
With three Wise Men
Traveling to find a Babe.
Today at Christmas time
I purchase dates and figs
Although my dad is gone,

My own children are grown
but the rubies, emeralds,
Camels and drifting sands
Yet materialize
And are as real to me now
As they were then
When I was a little girl in the mountains
Who found dates and figs under the tree
On wind-whipped snowy
Star-filled December
Christmas nights.

Inge Logenburg Kyler, December 7, 1993

Christmas Night

A misplaced star seems tied to Earth
as voices echo in the night.
Then speaks a messenger from God—
That shepherds need not fright.
Their terrors cease. The night has peace.
God's Son has come to Earth!
And sign we now, and hold we cheer,
and praise the Savior's birth.

Robert B. Ward, December 18, 1990

Christmas Festiveness

Pine boughs bend, laden
with new-fallen snow
as holiday shoppers
rush to and fro
with arms full of parcels
to share their good cheer
for an old-fashioned Christmas
and a Happy New Year!

Helena K. Stefanski, December 18, 1990

Hold On To Christmas
Hold Christmas
in your mind,
the expectation
bringing joy.

Hold Christmas
in your hand,
letting the joy
flow in every job.

Hold Christmas
to your ear,
the joyous carols
bringing harmony.

Hold Christmas
in your heart
and the wonder
of its love
will be a true
rejoicing!

Elizabeth Searle Lamb, December 3, 1985

Christmas
There's more, much more to Christmas
Than candlelight and cheer;
It's the spirit of sweet friendship
That brightens all the year;
It's thoughtfulness and kindness,
It's hope reborn again,
For peace, for understanding
And for good will to men!

Churchman, December 22, 1951

Father's Christmas Trees

Father bought the strangest trees!
I thought when I was little—
Skinny, needles dropping by my knees
Sometimes open in the middle...
He would say, "I'm sorry for them
All pushed aside, alone, unwanted;
And he'd adopt them like some orphan
Over protests, calm, undaunted.
And then would come a miracle
For dressed in gold and tiny lights
And lovely handmade ornaments,
The trees shone forth on Christmas night
Transfigured, glorious and grand,
Revealing hidden majesty—
From Father's heart and artful hands
Were fashioned perfect Christmas trees.

Judy DeVivo, December 20, 1983

Christmas

His name day
came and went
those years
unmarked
except for Mary's
tears, the stab
of pain that pierced
her heart.

No songs, no sweetened cake
upon the hearth.
No gifts;
no reason seen
to give, to celebrate
such common season.

CHRISTMAS WITH KATE

No calendar
to mark
his birth,
yet the whole far
Earth now
counts its days,
fills sky
with praise
because he came.
This Day
we call his
Name.

B.R. Culbertson, December 21, 1993

Christmas Tree
Sweet memories now trim this Christmas tree
That gleams behind the pane for all to see.
Those fragile bells of Austrian glass recall
That dream vacation trip one lovely fall.
The shiny paper star, one point not straight,
Was made by Dave when he was barely 8.
The paint on wooden flute and drum is dim
From annual polishing by Sue and Jim.
This tree is green and trimmed with yesterday,
Blessed by the love of Him to whom we pray.

Doris Louise Alsup, December 25, 1979

Legends & Customs

Chapter 8

AMERICANS SHARE MANY ethnic backgrounds, and our rich cultural heritage is seldom more evident than during the Christmas season. The customs of the French, Scandinavian, German, Spanish and English are just of few of those that flavor our celebrations. From midnight masses to our beloved Christmas trees, many of our traditions have their roots in the customs of other lands.

I have enjoyed the readers' letters that share the origins of these customs, as well as those that they have discovered while living and traveling in other lands. I hope that you, too, will enjoy learning about these holiday customs from around the world.

Customs Of Other Lands

There are many Christmas superstitions that are a mixture of ancient pagan and early Christian rites from many lands.

Families in Scandinavia leave their beds and sleep on the floor on Christmas Eve because of an old superstition that ghosts of the family dead revisit the old homestead that eve.

Bohemian peasants believe that plucking embers from the Christmas fire and throwing them into the wells is a certain safe-guard against drought and famine in their country.

In Greece, it is believed that on Christmas Eve the trees and plants—especially those on the banks of the Jordan—bow in rever-ence to the Savior.

To break before Christmas time the earthen jar called the "family pig," in which savings have accumulated, is considered unlucky in Holland.

An ancient superstition in England is that unless horses and cattle are given double rations of feed on Christmas Day, misfor-tune will follow.

There is a legend that Christ's thorny crown was made of holly and that the berries sprang from drops of His blood.

MRS. F.D. December 25, 1937

Mistletoe Legend

Why do we kiss under mistletoe? Because it is the emblem of love. Loki, one of the Scandinavian deities, hated Balder the Beautiful, who was immune from any weapons that originated in water, soil, air or fire. Since mistletoe is a parasite of the cedar tree, Loki made an arrow of mistletoe and killed Balder. But Balder the Beautiful was restored to life, and the mistletoe was given to the goddess of love to see that it was only used for love and never for hate.

Therefore, everyone who passes under mistletoe is entitled to a kiss to prove the former instrument of hate is now the emblem of love.

MRS. A.R. December 20, 1930

Christmas Symbols

Hundreds of years ago at Christmastide, the ancient Druids formed long and solemn processions and went to gather mistletoe from the woods. They wore white coats in their ceremonies, and the mistletoe was divided among all the people and hung over the doorways to bring good fortune.

The Yule log has an old, old story. Hundreds of years ago the Saxons held their winter festivals and called them Yuletide. In Serbia, the father cuts down the oak for his Yule log and throws grain on it. He believes that the number of sparks that fly indicates how many farm animals will be born during the year.

As you hang your mistletoe and light your Yule logs, think back! Remember what these symbols meant to people centuries ago in other lands.

IOWA. December 24, 1949

First Christmas Card

A 16-year-old English lad in the year 1842, while serving as a London engraver's apprentice, designed the world's first Christmas card.

His name was William Maw Egley, and the quaint skating scene was sketched on gleaming copper. William's card did not meet with success because the English preferred to use their "Christmas letter," as was their custom. Although they ridiculed the idea as "too unconventional," the card proved to be the forerunner of one of the more colorful Christmas customs.

Years later, during the second Great International Exposition in London, a publisher again introduced the Christmas card, this time with great success. Christmas cards with religious designs were first published in Ireland in 1875.

The English lad's card carried the greeting we still find popular in cards today—"A Merry Christmas and a

HAPPY NEW YEAR." December 24, 1949

There's Music For Everyone

There's Christmas music to fit every age group and every mood. As a child, I thrilled with singing the carols at school and church programs. Later, as a teacher, these same Christmas carols were even more lovely and meaningful as I taught my children to sing them joyfully.

Hearing the Christmas records from our local courthouse tower during December is a happy reminder that I must hasten with shopping, for it gives me a satisfied feeling that everything is on schedule.

Holiday baking and arranging decorations throughout the house go much better to the merry tunes on the stereo. When friends stop by, we are renewed by the soft melodies of Christmas selections as we reminisce and relax with a cup of tea.

When I am 80, if I am fortunate enough to live that long, I am sure that Christmas music will carry me back through active decades to relive busy Christmas seasons with treasured

MEMORIES. December 15, 1970

Christmas Stories

At Valley Forge, George Washington had a baked potato for Christmas dinner—no more. He shared the fate of his men, and upon contemplating the potato he said, "Well, this is not so bad when you think what we are fighting for." His was certainly an example of spiritual courage on physical emptiness.

Different indeed is this story about Benjamin Franklin, who decided, way back in 1750, to kill the Christmas turkey by means of the latest thing, electricity. He proceeded to do so for the edification of some of his close friends. Well, it seems that in all the excitement, Doctor Franklin forgot to let go of something. The current missed the bird completely, giving our hero one of the "shocks" of his life. And the joke apparently was not on the turkey.

HISTORY LOVER. December 20, 1941.

What Christmas Songs?

Fill each blank with the right word and you'll have familiar lines from old Christmas songs. Allow yourself 6 points for each correct filler. If you average 48 points that's fair; 60 is good; 72 or better is excellent.

1. "I heard the bells on Christmas Day. Their old familiar ——— play." Longfellow.
2. "For Christmas comes but ——— a year." Macfarren.
3. "The stockings were hung by the ——— with care." Moore.
4. "Peace on Earth and mercy mild, God and ——— reconciled." Wesley.
5. "Christmas is coming, the ——— are getting fat." Old rhyme.
6. "The hopes and fears of all the years, Are met in ——— tonight." Brooks.
7. "The world in solemn stillness lay, To hear the ——— sing." Sears.
8. "The angel of the ——— came down, And glory shown around." Tate.
9. "As ——— was a-walking, He heard an angel sing." Old carol.
10. "Away in a ———, no crib for a bed." Luther.
11. "Little Jack ——— sat in a corner, eating his Christmas pie." Traditional.
12. "God rest ye ——— gentlemen, let nothing you dismay." Traditional.
13. "Today the Prince of ——— is born." J.R. Lowell.
14. "Little Jesus was Thou shy, Once and just so ——— as I?" Fr. Thompson.
15. "The Christ-child stood at ———'s knee. His hair was like a crown." Chesterton.

Answers:
1. carols
2. once
3. chimney
4. sinners
5. geese
6. Thee
7. angels
8. Lord
9. Joseph
10. manger
11. Horner
12. merry
13. Peace
14. small
15. Mary

103

First Christmas Card

When young Henry Cole, a clerk in an English records office, sat down in December, 1846, to compose a Christmas message to a friend, he had an idea that changed Christmas for millions of people. He decided to send a greeting card with a picture—the first Christmas card historians have been able to authenticate.

Cole—later Sir Henry Cole, educational reformer and illustrator of children's stories—got an artist friend, J.C. Horsley, member of the Royal Academy, to design the card for him.

Horsley's drawing shows a merry family party in the center. On two side panels figures represent two acts of charity: feeding and clothing the poor.

The words of the greeting are those still most popular: "A Merry Christmas and a Happy New Year to You." The idea of the Christmas card spread quickly in England and soon became popular in America and on the Continent.

One of the most famous collections of Christmas cards is that of Jonathon King. He collected between six and seven tons of cards, over 163,000 varieties contained in 700 volumes.

A.T.H. December 22, 1951

It's Interesting To Know

It's interesting to know:

Our first Santa Claus was pictured as a tall, thin individual, unlike the plump rosy-cheeked modern Santa.

The first Christmas card was sent a little over 100 years ago.

In Belgium, a white sheet is spread on the floor. Sweets are thrown on this, and Santa enters as the children scramble for them.

In Holland the children set out wooden shoes or baskets for gifts, leaving food in these containers for the Saint's white horse.

The Mexican Christmas celebration is a very religious one that begins December 16 and ends on Christmas Eve.

The Pilgrims considered the celebration of Christmas sinful.

MARIA. December 25, 1948

Words On Christmas

Let's stop for a moment amid the hustle and bustle of this joyous holiday season and consider the meaning of some of the words associated with this time of year.

To me, it is interesting to know something of the background of some of the names, so let's consider the word Christmas.

This is two separate nouns—Christ and mas. The former is from the Greek *Christos*, meaning anointed; the latter is a Hebrew word, *mas*, meaning a tribute. The literal meaning of Christmas is a festival in memory of Christ.

I wonder how many people know that the name of Santa Claus originated in the early colonial days of our country? It comes from a mispronunciation of the Dutch name for St. Nicholas—San Nik'laas.

St. Nicholas was a real person, who lived during the fourth century in Asia Minor. In Russia he was regarded as the guardian saint of children.

Kris Kringle is the name by which the jolly old fellow who comes down the chimney on Christmas Eve is called among the German people.

Yule is an old Norse name for a festival held at the Christmas season. The familiar word, yuletide, is used by the Scandinavian people as well as by ourselves.

Noël is a French word meaning a Christmas carol.

MARTHA. December 15, 1945

Don't Miss The Mince!

Don't miss the mince at Christmas time. Don't miss it, that is, if you are superstitious and believe in the old Yorkshire saying, "In as many houses as you eat mince pie in the 12 days of Christmas, so many happy months are assured during the coming year."

If there is any truth in this superstition, then even the most conscientious weight-watchers should not steer clear of what is generally accepted as America's No. 1 Christmas

DESSERT. December 10, 1949

An Angel's Tears Began The Bells

Bells ring and jingle, tinkle and peal, all around the world during the Christmas season. They make music seem merrier, hearts lighter.

I once read a fanciful story of a little angel who wanted to sing in the heavenly choir on the night Jesus was born, but he couldn't sing on key. As he sat sad and lonely, watching the angels make their glorious announcement to the shepherds, a tear rolled down his cheek.

The falling tear struck a bell tied to the neck of a lamb, and the bell rang with a clear, crisp "ting" so lovely that all hearing it paused for a moment. The little angel became so excited he rushed about ringing every bell he could find to tell everyone that the Savior was born.

Since that time bells are heard and seen at Christmas to tell the "good tidings of great joy." Is it any wonder that the bells at Christmas make the whole world seem a little

GAYER. December 21, 1971

Trick Or Treaters On Christmas Eve

I've always associated trick-or-treat here in the states with Halloween, but according to my homemaker's club yearbook, they had it on Christmas Eve in the early days of our nation after the Moravian Germans came to Pennsylvania.

The Dutch housewives were busy all day before Christmas Eve cracking nuts, beating eggs and grating chocolate for Christmas cookies and baking them by the washbuckets full. They wanted enough for guests and *belsnickels*, the Christmas Eve trick-or-

TREATERS. November 11, 1975

Christmas In India

I have had the divine pleasure of seeing your paper and reading with hearty interest your letters from women all over. I wonder if your readers would like to hear about Christmas in my homeland, India.

106

One week before the holiday of Christmas we fast by not eating animal food, and on the last day we eat no food at all. On Christmas Eve we take communion. All families are present at this service, and the young children read from the Book of Daniel.

After services we all return to our houses and light candles, and the members of the family break their fast. *Pilav*, a rice food, is eaten abundantly. As soon as we have all had our fill we go to the rooftops and sing lustily, "Rejoice and be glad. Open your bag and fill you handkerchiefs. Hallelujah, Hallelujah!"

We fill our handkerchiefs with raisins and nuts or fried wheat and put some money in them. In the evening the priest visits the houses of the mourning in his parish and repeats a good prayer.

On Christmas night in our town the engaged young men bring trays to their fiancées. On the trays are 12 pieces of cake, a candle, nine eggs, some raisins, a plate of *halva* (a sweetmeat), and a box of *hina* (sweet-smelling oil for the hair and hands).

Early the next morning church services are held, and all hasten to be present. The ceremony of pouring out the holy water of baptism (*meron*) then takes place. Glasses are dipped into the blessed water. Some people take the water home to be mixed with pure earth. It is then kept in a special vessel for purifying purposes. During Christmas week when people visit each other, they greet one another with this saying: "Happy Blessing-of-the-Water. May you live to see the holy and vast Resurrection."

Christmas in my mother country is a sacred thing, but I love, too, the Christmases in the United States. I have had but one happy experience, but I look forward again this year to celebrating the birth of the babe in Bethlehem.

How I long deep in my heart for peace to settle over our earth once more—a peace in the hearts of your people and my people now and for always. The Prince of Peace shall come again all over the whole wide world. In India, in Korea, in Japan, in Europe, everywhere; there shall be the glad tidings once more. I shall keep peace in my heart

FOREVER. December 16, 1950

Christmas Folklore

Wet strawbands tied around orchard trees on Christmas Eve will make them fruitful.

If a shirt be spun, woven, or sewed by a chaste maid on Christmas Eve, it will withstand lead and steel.

As often as the cock crows on Christmas Eve, the quarter of corn will be as dear.

If one wanders into the winter corn on holy Christmas Eve, he will hear what will happen in the village that year.

Residents of Madrid, Spain, eat 12 grapes at midnight on Christmas Eve for good luck.

In Silesia it is believed that a child born on Christmas Day will grow up to be either a thief or a lawyer.

AUNT KIT. December 21, 1946

Christmas Superstitions

In the Netherlands it is thought that nothing sown on Christmas Eve will perish, even though the seeds be sown in the snow.

In Spain everyone is admonished to treat cows kindly on Christmas Eve because they believe that the cattle breathed on the Christ Child to keep him warm.

If you eat a raw egg before going to bed on Christmas Eve you will be able to carry heavy loads from then on, according to the people of Ireland.

When a Bohemian wife burns a Christmas cake she believes she will die within a year.

In Ireland it is believed that the gates of paradise are always open on Christmas Eve. Dying then, one would not go to purgatory.

Folks in several countries believe it is unlucky to launder a Christmas gift before presenting it as it takes out the good luck. They also think that a washcloth used to groom horses on Christmas Day will cause them to grow fat.

MRS. P.V.S. December 17, 1949

Christmas Beliefs

Do you share these Christmas beliefs?

The luckiest person in the house will be the first one who opens the door to let Christmas in.

The angels leave heaven on Christmas Eve to awaken the infants from their sleep and carry them to Paradise to sing a carol for the Christ Child. Then they tuck them safely into their beds again.

The Blessed Mother and her babe or some stranger may rap on your door on Christmas Eve and ask for food and shelter. Whoever hears the knock has good luck.

A lighted candle in your window during the Christmas season will help the Christ Child find

HIS WAY. December 15, 1951

An Old Christmas Legend

According to an ancient legend the animals in our barns receive the gift of speech in the quiet, solemn hours of Christmas night. The legend tells us they speak because of the King who once made their manger and the lowly stable holy the night the Star appeared in faraway Bethlehem.

Legend tells us, too, that at the stroke of midnight every animal in our stables will bend his knee in honor and reverence for the One who hallowed their home by making it His humble birthplace.

While children lay dreaming of the joys of the morrow, it would be interesting some Christmas night to creep out to the barnyard and see or fancy that we see all this at that reverential hour. But as day breaks the charm ceases. The children arise to clamor about the tree. Shouts of "Merry Christmas" and the opening of gifts absorb our attention. The goose is stuffed and popped into the oven. Relatives are welcomed, and eyes sparkle. And our faithful animal friends continue their toiling lives of honest, dependable service.

E.R. December 25, 1948

Views Cross In Sky On Christmas

As you folks enter into the spirit of Christmas—with snow and winter weather—we head gaily for the beach, as days become longer and warmer. Spring blossoms are over for another year and summer flowers—petunias, phlox, zinnias and such—are taking their place in a riot of color.

We always hope Christmas Day will be a fine one, not too hot for eating midday dinner, but somehow it never really matters. Christmas appetites seem to be the same the world over no matter what the weather. As a family, we commence our Christmas with 6 a.m. holy communion at the Anglican church of St. John the Baptist. Then home for a quick breakfast so we can open the beautifully wrapped presents beneath the gaily decorated Christmas tree. During the morning, folks pop in to help us celebrate. I keep basting the turkey to keep those wonderful juices in place.

Our dinner still closely follows old English tradition, with poultry, pork and hot vegetables, followed by Christmas plum pudding and brandy sauce, nuts, sweets, etc. For good Australia's sake we also serve fruit salad and ice cream.

Some folks prefer to take salads to the beach and swim, water ski, or just bask lazily in the sunshine. I feel there is all the rest of the summer for that but only one Christmas Day.

The Sunday evening before Christmas is always welcomed in with candlelight carol services held in churches, city squares and gardens. On Boxing Day—the day after Christmas—the best of our horses are seen at big races, and the Sydney to Hobart yacht race gets under way.

As you end Christmas Day within your homes, well-warmed against the cold outside, perhaps you could in spirit come with me out into the soft stillness of the summer night and look up into the heavens, while I point out to you those lovely stars that make up our beautiful Southern Cross that can only be seen in the Southern Hemisphere. May peace indeed come to each and every
ONE OF YOU. December 20-27, 1966

Foods 'Round The World

Did you ever stop to think of all the foods other nations prepare at Christmas time? I didn't myself until I started a little research. It was interesting to find that the people of Rumania make thin, dry wafers that are baked to represent the swaddling clothes of the Christ Child. Because they are flavorless, they are eaten with honey and syrup. Another special dish is stuffed pig's stomach.

In Norway, as the Christmas porridge was served in earlier times, one of the people in the room fired a gun as a sort of salutation and to drive away the evil spirits, gnomes and sprites that wished to seize upon the beloved porridge.

In Ukrania, during a 39-day fast, no meat is eaten until Christmas Eve, when a 12-course dinner is served, one course for each apostle. Served at this dinner are buckwheat-and-mushroom soup, prune pancakes in flax cabbage, fish, bread and nuts.

In Germany, the crumbs from the Christmas table—when shaken on the soil, cause a little plant known as the *Crumbwort* to spring up. This little plant is said to have great healing powers.

In England it is said that bread baked on Christmas day will never become moldy.

When I think of our fruit cakes, fancy Christmas cookies, roast turkey and all the other goodies, I wonder if folks around the world celebrate as we do, spending hours in the kitchen for weeks before Christmas. I have a feeling they do, for after all, no matter where the spirit of Christmas shines, it lives in the hearts of men, women and children, as it does in mine.

HOLLY. December 25, 1948

Polish Tradition

My parents both came from Poland, and we continue to observe a Christmas tradition from that country. On Christmas Eve we have a family reunion for the *Wilia* supper. The table is fixed with a thin layer of hay under the white tablecloth in memory of the Christ Child in the manger. When the first star appears in the sky the family gathers at the table. Before sitting down, all the family, beginning with the eldest, break a piece of the traditional wafer called *oplatek* and exchange good wishes.

The supper consists of seven strictly meatless courses. Polish dishes are served. It is a tradition most dear to my heart. I hope my children will carry on putting hay under the tablecloth on Christmas Eve. The cloth is left there throughout Christmas Day with goodies on the table for visiting

GUESTS. December 18, 1956

Christmas Customs

To make our Christmas special with five youngsters ages 11 to 2 years, we are celebrating customs of other countries. This year we will celebrate a Mexican Christmas with a piñata. We hope to experience as many of one country's customs each year as possible, including their native foods. Denmark and England will be next, since they are our ancestors'

COUNTRIES. December 1-8, 1964

Kissing Is Part Of Lore

Mistletoe's shiny green leaves and bright red berries, along with the associated kissing custom, combine to make a popular and interesting Yuletide decoration. Many do not know the tradition of kissing under the mistletoe is deeply rooted in folklore and religious rites of other lands.

Early Christians held the theory that the mistletoe plant once had been a large tree. They believed when the wood from the mistletoe was used for the cross upon which Christ died, the tree diminished in size from shame.

Even today in many countries, mistletoe is hung in homes to protect loved ones from harm. According to early settlers, mistletoe holds supernatural powers for good.

Men and women who kiss beneath the mistletoe are thought to profess deep and abiding

LOVE. December 17, 1985

Roast Pig Feast

My husband is an Army staff sergeant, and we were stationed in Hawaii the past two years. There they celebrate Christ's birthday by shooting fireworks and enjoying a luau.

A luau, or feast as we know it, consists of several different dishes, the main one being roast pig. To roast the pig, they fill it with red-hot lava rocks and wrap it in banana and ti leaves. They place more hot lava rocks over the pig, which is placed in a hole in the ground. The pig and rocks are covered with dirt making an earthen oven called an *imu*. With the pig, they bake bananas and yams. Poi and raw fish are two other dishes served.

We found it hard to feel any Christmas spirit since the weather was so hot and humid—like a Kansas summer. Even the Christmas trees lost their pine scent since they were shipped from the States and had to be specially treated to last through the holidays. Our Hawaiian Christmases were colorful, but we are happy and thankful to be spending this Christmas at home in

KANSAS. December 24, 1957

CHRISTMAS WITH KATE

114

Mistletoe Romances

Chapter 9

MAYBE IT'S THE mistletoe. Or it could be the general feeling of good will in the air. Whatever the cause, the holiday season seems to be a perfect time for falling in love. Readers who have been bitten by the Christmas lovebug have sent in wonderful stories that recount how an unexpected Christmas guest or a holiday decorating party set the scene for a romance that extended far beyond the holidays.

As you read these romantic tales, remember— it's never too late for the mistletoe to spark some holiday romance, even for those who have shared many Christmases together.

Doll For Christmas

It was Kay's first Christmas without her mamma. And she was 7 years old. How well I remembered another little girl, just 7 years old, who had wanted a doll, but because her relatives were so grief-stricken over their recent bereavement, they forgot about the child and Christmas.

Somehow I couldn't get it out of my mind, so I bought the doll for Kay. It had adorable golden curls and eyes that went to sleep. Then I wondered how I'd ever get it to her. Me, an old maid (well, anyway I was 30), taking a doll to a little girl whose father was the most eligible widower in town would set every tongue wagging. So I sent my neighbor's little girl to do it. She must have told who sent it, for that night at the Community Christmas Tree, before everybody in town, Kay's father came to me and thanked me most graciously, and Kay showed her own appreciation by having the doll hugged tightly in her arms.

Yes, I'm buying another doll for Kay this Christmas. You guessed it. She's my little girl now.

KANSAS. December 26, 1942

Under The Mistletoe

Just why my mother, who is really one of the best-hearted, kindest, most thoughtful of women, should have been so set against my getting married, I could never understand. Just to illustrate how fine she is, I must tell you that she always invites some stranger or poor family to share Christmas dinner with us. Last year, as usual, she extended her invitation to the Smiths, who had recently moved to our neighborhood.

"We'd love to come," Mrs. Smith accepted, and added, "my niece may be visiting us then. You wouldn't mind if I brought her?"

Naturally, mother couldn't refuse, although she knew this niece was unmarried, and she disliked having young, single girls at our house. She may have been somewhat comforted by the reflection that Mrs. Smith is a very thin, prim woman with an underslung jaw—hardly likely to have a beautiful niece.

116

If mother didn't want me to get married, she gave one too many Christmas dinners. Niece Sally Jo turned out to be a laughing, lovable scamp with a round, dimpled chin and dark blue eyes. Even poor, bashful, mother-complexed me grew bold enough to catch her under the mistletoe. And now, after six months of having Sally Jo for a daughter-in-law, even poor, disappointed, son-complexed mother is reconciled.

HAPPY JACK. December 19, 1936

'Twas Short But Sweet

"Arlie, will you marry me here next Christmas?" It came as suddenly as that: right out of a blue sky in a nutshell—time, place 'n' everything.

It was Christmas Eve, and our gang was decorating the church for the community tree. Harold, my lifelong pal, and I were working in a corner by ourselves. There were mistletoe berries in his tousled hair, soot and ink on his face, dust and grime on his clothes and hands. But—there was lovelight in his eyes as he made his public proposal.

I wasn't so sudden in my acceptance, but anyway, we are decorating a little tree for a tiny tot this year.

HAROLD'S PAL. December 24, 1932

Really Unique Gift

Since so many folks are writing to "Heart of the Home" about their greatest thrills and surprises, please let me add mine to the list. Mine I shall call "My Bestest Christmas Present."

A young man and I had been keeping company for several months and were planning to be married sometime in the near future. As I had no parents of my own, I was often a guest in the home of my boyfriend's parents, who were lovely people and so hospitable.

Christmas came, and I spent Christmas Eve in my friend's home so as to be there the next morning. Early Christmas morning we all arose and gathered around the Christmas tree to find what Santa had left us. After we had ooh-ed and ah-ed about our gifts, I went into the kitchen to wash so I could help with breakfast. I heard someone come into the room. When I looked around, there stood my boyfriend with a Christmas card hung around his neck. On it was written: "To Our Daughter, from Mother and Father."

I believe that was the happiest moment of my life. In all the Christmases past, and all those to come, he was and shall always be the "bestest" Christmas present I could ever have.

And I guess I oughta know, cause ever since that Christmas we've been Mr. and Mrs. Santa Claus.

DAUGHTER-IN-LAW. December 16, 1939

A Day To Remember

The Christmas I like to remember best? The Christmas I spent in Denver. A very cold and snowy Christmas. The charmed and beautiful Christmas of fifteen years ago. The Christmas when my life loyalty took shape and I accepted a lovely sparkling diamond to wear on my left hand.

We have spent fourteen Christmases since then around our own fireside. Three children have joined us with their lively enthusiasm and joyous laughter. Each Christmas is richer in meaning than the one that preceded it. Because I was young, I was very sure I was doing the right thing in regard to my future—but oh! I was so much wiser than I knew that snowy Christmas in Denver

FIFTEEN YEARS AGO. December 23, 1944

Happy Home Glows With Christmas Spirit

When I was growing up, my home was many miles from a paved highway and was reached only by slow and careful driving over graveled, rutty roads. However, we owned a couple of trucks, as well as a late-model car, and always had transportation to high school activities, 4-H meetings, club meetings, etc. So I never gave our location much thought, except to enjoy its beauty.

In contrast, my husband's family lived only a few yards from the highway and about 15 miles from town. From chance remarks he's made in the last few years, I've learned that he thought his family had quite an advantage over other farm families that were unlucky enough to live "way back in the sticks" or "in the backwoods."

This attitude was brought rather forcefully to my attention last Christmas, when I listened in open-mouthed surprise to a description my husband gave our children of the first time he drove past my home. It, too, was during the Christmas season on a dark, cold night.

After driving for miles without seeing any lights, his whole family was surprised and delighted to swing around the corner of a pitch-dark road to see our Christmas tree all lit up in one window and a lovely wreathed electric candle in another. We had a large two-story house, and the warm glow of a happy family busily preparing for the holidays shone from every window. He said they slowed the car and finally came to a halt, just sitting and gazing for a moment before driving on.

I didn't know whether to laugh or be indignant at discovering his attitude. But all in all, he must have thought well enough of that "backwoods" girl by the Christmas lights that he asked her to MARRY HIM. December 4, 1973

How About It, Mister

Want to give your wife a special sort of gift? Then why not a "date" such as you used to have—just for one evening. Dress up in your very best and tell her—the way you used to—that she looks swell. Leave the kids at home.

At the risk of her thinking you've been up to something, buy her a box of candy, take in a good show, and go to a restaurant for dinner.

She'll tell you it was the nicest gift she ever received. ONE MISSUS. December 6, 1941

Soldier Wins Girlfriend With Kiss

My boyfriend and I were at a Christmas party when a young soldier came up to me and asked, "Has your boyfriend kissed you under the mistletoe yet?"

I said no, and the soldier said, "Then he is an idiot and you shouldn't marry him." He grabbed me and kissed me, saying, "If I had a girlfriend like you, I'd hang mistletoe up all year long."

I broke up with my boyfriend and wrote to the soldier. He went to Vietnam, and I waited three years to see him again. When he came home at Christmas we got married. I carried mistletoe in my bridal bouquet.

We've been married 24 years and have five children. I'm so glad I met this wonderful man under the
MISTLETOE! December 19, 1989

Liked His Cooking

It was snowing and sleeting when Aunt Ocie arrived on Christmas Eve to spend the holidays with us on our farm in the Ozarks. She had lived in the city all her life, and I know our ways seemed queer to her, but she did not let on. Our lack of bathing facilities and other conveniences city dwellers take for granted seemed to amaze her at first. But soon she caught on to our ways and seemed to enjoy herself.

On Christmas Eve the children hung up their stockings in traditional style and went off to bed early. We grownups sat around the wood fire until midnight cracking nuts, telling jokes and reminiscing about the past. Our good neighbor Uncle Bob dropped in, and we introduced him to Aunt Ocie, who had never married, she said, because the ones she wanted didn't want her and vice-versa.

Finally, one by one, the family drifted off to bed, leaving Uncle Bob and Aunt Ocie talking and laughing like old friends. No one would guess that she was a city-bred woman and he a hillbilly bachelor.

Next day, as Aunt Ocie helped me put the finishing touches on our holiday feast, I noticed a sparkle in her eyes. It was easy to see that she had found a new interest. I did not say anything, and none of the others teased her about Uncle Bob. As the family was gathering around the table I heard a gentle knock at the back door. It was Uncle Bob, standing there with a huge bowl of steaming hot, fresh-cooked pig knuckles and homemade sauerkraut. I knew he had killed hogs the day before, and I knew he was a kind, generous soul, but I was not prepared for this.

"Made these myself," he grinned. "I want Miss Ocie to taste 'em."

I insisted that he come in and enjoy Christmas dinner with us. He seemed very happy and thanked me effusively. I seated him next to my smiling Aunt Ocie.

This year we are planning on having Christmas at their house, since Aunt Ocie is now

MRS. BOB. December 13, 1952

Reversing The Order

Vera and Joe had been going together so long their friends had ceased to speculate as to the ultimate outcome. Their romance was worn threadbare and taken for granted, and they were generally treated like old married folks at social gatherings in the community.

One snowy Christmas Eve, Vera came rushing into the kitchen where Sally and I were working over a pin-feathered turkey, shouting hysterically, "We've done it! We've done it!"

"Done what?" Sally turned, a butcher knife poised in the air. "Done what?"

"Adopted a baby!"

About that time, Joe sauntered in proudly holding a big basket, wherein a beautiful dark-haired baby boy—just three days old—slept peacefully, tucked snugly beneath a woolly blanket.

We looked on speechless, for after all we were a respectable, conventional, old-fashioned bunch, and we couldn't grasp the situation.

"Oh, don't look so dumfounded," Vera went on. "Joe and I have thought this thing out. We are going to start our married life right from the start with a baby. We are getting up in years, and what's a sweeter Christmas present than a precious baby? Joe and I went to a private maternity hospital and selected this little fellow, and we're going to have the time of our lives. It's 3 o'clock now, Joe—time for his bottle."

That afternoon—amidst their big circle of friends—Vera and Joe were married in the little parsonage, while little Davey Lee lay quietly in his basket nearby, blinking his sleepy eyes at the minister.

B.H. December 24, 1932

Just For Me

My Christmas wish is entirely selfish. I guess it should be for world peace—in Vietnam, co-existence with Russia, peace in our own country—with all men living as brothers. But my own special private wish is for myself.

I wish I could meet that special man who all the romantic novels indicate was created just for me. I don't care if he's dark or fair, heavy or slim, short or tall. The only requirements are gentleness, compassion, a sense of humor and honesty; he must like children and have love for me. I want his eyes to light up when he sees me the way I've seen other men and women look at one another.

What I want most of all is to become a complete woman, to have a home of my own and

CHILDREN. December 16, 1969

Off A Christmas Tree

It happened several Christmases ago. We were preparing for the party in the church basement. I was up on the stepladder fixing the decorations at the top of the tree. How it happened, I never knew, but somehow I lost my balance. With a scream I landed in the arms of an eligible bachelor. Trying to cover my confusion I gasped, "You sure caught a Christmas package." Amid the laughter he answered, "And believe me, I'm going to try to keep it, too."

We had a June wedding.

A READER. December 24, 1932

Still Treasures Little Gold Locket

The Christmas I remember best was the year I was a teenager in high school in the early '40s, when I received my first real gift from my boyfriend.

It was a dainty, beautiful gold locket to hold his picture, and quite unexpected. I'll never forget the thrill of putting it on and how it felt around my neck. What made it even more valuable to me was realizing that it was bought at a sacrifice to him, as no one had much money in those days. I was hardly aware of the Christmas program that day at school because I was in such a state of bliss.

After the war, I married a fine fellow, and we will celebrate our silver wedding anniversary next June. However, nothing he has given me in all those years has ever equalled the thrill of my little gold locket. I have it yet. It is worn, but still

TREASURED. December 16, 1969

Roses And "That Man"

After reading the following episode, you can draw your own conclusions about how many times I received flowers from my husband during the 25 years of our married life. This doesn't necessarily mean he is a brute, or inconsiderate, but he just does not associate flowers with the living.

Last Christmas our daughter came home from Denver to spend the Christmas holidays. As a surprise Christmas gift to her, the best boyfriend from there had ordered a bouquet of flowers to be delivered to her on Christmas morn. When the messenger from the local florist shop rang the doorbell on that morning, it so happened we were all still in bed except my husband. As he opened the door, the boy thrust a bouquet of red roses into his hand. He took one look at the flowers and said, "You must have the wrong address, there isn't anyone dead here," and passed them back to the boy. By this time, fortunately, Dorothy was wide awake. She quickly came to the door and retrieved her roses.

HER MOM. December 22, 1945

123

The Man Got His Answer

Last Christmas Eve a special messenger brought to the door a box of chocolates tied with red and green ribbon. Under the ribbon was a note:

"I remembered the kind of candy you like, Margaret. I remember that you don't like to be left alone at night and that you can't believe a man loves you if he doesn't kiss you goodbye every morning. I remember that you don't like lies—even little, white ones. If I promise to remember all these things always, will you forget I was a terrible failure as a husband and give me a second chance? Jack."

After hearing from him like that after three long months of separation, I prayed: "Lord, don't let me be dreaming." I didn't realize the freckled messenger boy was still waiting until I met his wide, curious eyes.

"The man who gave me that, lady," he said, "he's waiting down at th' corner if there's any answer..."

Trembling, I scribbled a line on a sheet of paper.

Now, after a whole year together again, Jack says he'll never forget how he felt when he read that line under the street lamp: "I remember you liked to find me waiting at the door when you came home."

MARGARET. December 25, 1937

Christmas Ring

The special Christmas gift that will always stand out in my memory is my wedding ring. You see, we were married in 1933, when times were hard and money scarce. A ring of any kind was out of the question. At the time I thought little about it, but later I secretly wished for a ring.

Lo and behold, 13 years and three children later my husband gave me a beautiful wedding ring for Christmas. Believe me, I was as proud and happy as any young bride could ever hope to be. My ring will always be my most treasured

GIFT. December 7-14, 1965

Ragged Blue Jeans For Christmas

I had been dating my husband-to-be for several months. One year he was stationed in Texas serving with the Army, and he was continually asking what I wanted for Christmas. One day I told him he could get me a pair of blue jeans, as mine were getting rather worn.

He came home on leave, and one day a lovely package appeared under the Christmas tree at my home. I pinched, shook and tried every conceivable way to peek. I had bought a bulky knit sweater for him, and the boxes were about the same size.

Shortly after midnight on Christmas Eve we agreed to open our packages. I excitedly tore the wrapping paper and ribbons off and pulled the box apart. Inside was a pair of faded, ragged blue jeans. They were the most dilapidated, worn pair you can imagine. Rising to the gag, I leaped up and paraded around laughing and holding them up for size.

After several minutes Kirk called my attention to the red ribbon tied to the front of the jeans. "Isn't that a pretty ribbon? I put a lot of work into that ribbon," he kept repeating. I agreed it was and began fingering the ribbon. It was fastened around the snap, and also fastened by the snap was a beautiful engagement ring!

That was the best pair of blue jeans I've ever owned, and that one Christmas will stand out from all others

FOREVER. December 21-28, 1965

Christmas Spark

At Christmas in 1924 I was going with a girl who was in a Christmas night play at church. I sat back with the crowd.

Somehow, I didn't know how or why, I leaned too far back in my chair and fell backwards. A girl sitting behind me grabbed me as I fell in her lap. Our eyes met, and that was IT! Neither of us said a word, but there was an understanding in our eyes.

I took the girl I went with home and told her I wouldn't be back because I was going to marry the other girl. On February 18 we did get married. That one look changed my outlook on girls—

before I looked into those eyes, girls were just someone to have fun with, but from then on, they were someone's sweetheart, to love and be loved.

I sure am glad I went to church that night. Since 1925, just to touch this girl who became my wife gives me a thrill. The years have been wonderful to both

OF US. December 18-25, 1962

Gets Engaged At The 10-Cent Store

"Let's go Christmas shopping," he said.

Even in Depression years people fell in love, so I reached for my worn coat, my empty purse and said, "Let's."

Up and down the street we walked, hand in hand, window shopping and dreaming.

"Let's go in," he said when we came to the 10-cent store. He pulled me over to the jewelry counter. "May we see that tray of rings, please?" he asked the clerk. "See one you like?" he asked.

"I love this sapphire. It's my birthstone," I said.

"But an engagement ring is supposed to be a diamond," he objected.

"Engagement!" I exclaimed. Everyone close turned and smiled.

"Someday I'll get you a real diamond—that is, if you'll marry me."

"Oh, I will, but I still want the sapphire for my engagement ring."

From his wallet he took out a dollar bill. "She'll wear the ring," he said to the clerk.

"MERRY CHRISTMAS."

Many of them have come and gone. He kept his word; I have a lovely diamond and gold band, but it is the dollar sapphire that holds the place of honor in my jewelry box. It symbolizes love, and that is

CHRISTMAS. December 18, 1973

Jolly Old Saint Nick

Chapter 10

H E'S CALLED BY many names—including Father Christmas, Kris Kringle and Saint Nicholas, just to name a few. Whatever name you choose for the jolly old elf dressed in red, he brings joy to children all around the world at Christmas time.

The legend of a kindly man who bestows gifts on children in December has both pagan and Christian roots. Through the centuries, they have melded together to create the character we in America know as Santa Claus.

Santa's image may continue to evolve, but the thrill he brings to the young and the young at heart will always be one of the joys of Christmas.

Puzzled Over Santa

When the couple next door was on their way home from a department store visit to Santa, their 6-year-old son said, "Tell me the truth, is there really a Santa Claus?"

"Don't you think so?" stalled his mother.

"Well, yes," answered the boy, "but tonight he had brown eyes, and last week when Grandma took me to see him his eyes were BLUE. December 13, 1977

Santa Receives Big Thank-You

Dear Santa,

Christmas Eve, along with cookies on the plate and sugar cubes for the reindeer, I want to leave you something else. The children who used to leave the cookies have long since gone. Only one grownup daughter sleeps upstairs, and she puts the cookies out more as a concession to her mother than to feed Santa. But I want to leave a thank-you letter with the cookies.

Thank you for all the Christmases that have made up my life. There are so many of them as I look back.

Thank you for the magic ones of my own childhood, especially the Christmas when my brother and I found the baby doll in the closet, then waited to see if it would be under the tree. When it was, it didn't spoil Christmas, it was only a great secret.

Thank you for the first Christmases when our own children were small. There was all the figuring, scrimping and saving we had to do to make Christmas special for little eyes and minds.

Thank you for the Christmases when the house was full and the "rafters rang" and there were so many we divided our present-giving between Christmas and Twelfth Night. And for the years when our sons in service sent back strange and beautiful gifts from other lands.

Thank you for the special Christmas when the Christmas Eve baby was born. She wasn't expected until January, but she must have decided to be part of the scene. I really didn't want to be away from the family that night, but Christmas was in the hospital, too. Carolers sang in the hall, and nurses carried the special brand-new baby down the hall to the nursery, calling, "New-born, new-born." Thank you for the babies who were having their first Christmas with bright solemn eyes reflecting the lights of the tree.

Thank you for the Christmases in between, as new families began and formed with their own traditions and customs.

Thank you for the quiet Christmases now, when most of the gay packages are wrapped and taken to other houses and grand-children's trees.

Thank you for every Christmas yet to come. And thank you most of all, Santa, that even after all these years, even with gray in my hair and all my wrinkles, I have never stopped believing in
YOU. December 21-28, 1976

Keep Up The Pretense

If any mothers doubt the joy of Santa Claus in the life of a child, let them ask one who has just gotten over the "believe in Santa" age. My son looked eagerly for old Santa each year until he was 8. On that particular Christmas Eve he was eager to help trim the tree that previously only old Santa Claus had been privileged to fix.

He patiently but silently waited for the sandman to take his smaller brother to sleep. Then he and I got out the trimmings and went to work. As the tree neared completion of its gay adornment, his small fingers worked slower and slower. Finally we were through, and he went slowly to bed, saying, "You can fill my stocking now."

The following morning he jumped briskly out of bed with his little brother, and from his "ahs" and "ohs," one would have thought he was seeing the tree for the first time.

Later he said to me, "You know, Mom, next year I am going to pretend I believe in Santa Claus and let you trim the tree alone. Let's not tell brother there isn't any Santa Claus for a long time. It's so much more fun to be surprised."
MISSOURI. December 13, 1941

Santa On Horseback

We had moved to the ranch with very little money, and not much but grit and determination to see us through the first winter. How we gloried in the orchard, the big garden spot and the virgin land waiting for the ox and plow.

By Christmas our small savings had dwindled to nothing. Snow lay deep on the mesas above the ranch. Christmas morning dawned sullenly. The kids had their noses plastered against the windows most of the day watching for Santa Claus. My heart grew heavier with each tick of the clock.

I couldn't explain to them that we were trying to make a go of it on the ranch that they might have a home. Toys and a lighted tree were the only language they wanted to hear then.

Around 3 o'clock it started to snow again. Suddenly the kids let out a yell: "Mom, Daddy, it's Santa Claus. He's coming up the trail."

I flung open the door to greet my neighbor and his wife whom I had seen only twice before. They had ridden down from their place on the mesa six miles away.

They led the pack horse up to the door and started handing me things. Apples, a big piece of beef, candy, toys for the kids. I don't suppose the cost of all of the things they brought would have amounted to a lot. Most of it they raised, but the thought that they had ridden through the cold six miles to see that two little kids could have Christmas brought back my faith in humanity.

To this day, the children don't picture Santa riding in a sleigh and driving reindeer. For them, he wears a sheepskin coat and rides a bay

COW-PONY. December 19, 1942

Santa Writes To Betty

Perhaps this may not be an alibi, but last Christmas I was "hard put" to get myself out of the jam I was in. My little girl had broken her dolly's head. I told her to write to old Santa and tell him to bring her a new one. In the meantime, we sent to a mail-

130

order house for one. When it arrived, just a week before Christmas, it was too large. I immediately sent it back for exchange, but Christmas Eve came and we were still without a head for poor dolly.

Before going to bed Betty put her doll on the davenport "where Santa could see it to put the new head on." What was I to do? I finally got the idea of leaving this letter in the dolly's hand: "Dear Betty—You did not tell me the size of your doll's head, and the one I brought was too large, so I'll send you one from Scissors & Sawbuck. Watch for the mailman. Santa."

Next morning instead of being disappointed, Betty was happy because she had a letter from Santa. In due time the mailman brought her the new head, which fit perfectly.

MOTHER. December 24, 1932

Gives Santa A Merry Chase

My father had to chase Santa Claus out of the house on Christmas morning.

Dad made quite a production of carrying out his task. He started at the top of the stairs, banging on pans and yelling at Santa. Then he rolled a washtub down the stairs, running after it and continuing to shout, "Get out of here, Santa!"

There followed a chase through the downstairs, with chairs being overturned and much noise. Then the front door slammed, and Dad called to us, "There, he's gone!" That was the signal for all of us children to scramble out of bed to see what Santa had left.

I was the youngest of five children. As a small child, I was frightened and concerned about Santa Claus. Everyone else seemed to enjoy this early morning chase immensely. Why would they treat Santa Claus like that, I wondered.

Of course, as I grew up I enjoyed Dad's antics as much as the others. Through the years we children enjoyed reminiscing about Dad's early Christmas-morning chase to get Santa Claus on his

WAY. December 17, 1985

Daddy Missed Santa

All the aunts, uncles and cousins were at Grandma's Christmas Eve. Too bad Daddy had to go to town for some medicine just before the fun started! The big boys were setting off fireworks for us little folks. We heard bells jingling, and the big kids began to yell that Santa Claus was coming through the orchard. How thrilled we were, and just a bit scared, too. Yes, there he was with his flashlight. He greeted us, and we followed him into the room where the big tree was loaded with pretty gifts.

He made all kinds of mistakes calling out our names and, of course, we laughed more than was necessary. I was standing by Mother, looking Santa over from head to foot. "Why, Mother, looky there. Santa's got shoes on just like Daddy's!"

"Yes, I believe he has. We'll have to tell Daddy," she said. Santa Claus had been gone about 30 minutes when Daddy came in, but he had plenty of little fellows to tell him about Santa's shoes.

FIFTEEN YEARS AGO. December 24, 1938

Santa Came For Sure

The faith of little children! We were all small, my brothers and I, and we had not come to know the meaning of our poverty, though such it would be considered today. Things such as Mother's low, sweet voice, Daddy's hearty laugh, and their mutual love of us were the ties that held us in a close-knit family unit. It was that delicious feeling of kinship that is one of the sweets of life.

That is why, when Mother gently hinted that Santa probably couldn't leave us very much in the way of toys on Christmas, we confidently said, "Oh, he won't forget us, Mother. We'll just put a candle in the window so he'll know we live here. He'll come. He always does."

Yes, Santa came. But at what sacrifice for our loving parents I can only guess. Now that I am grown up I realize something of the hardship of those homesteading days in the West

FIFTY YEARS AGO. December 21, 1946

Bicycles Prove Santa Is Real

Our three young sons had been wanting bicycles for a long time. Dick, 9, had a paper route, and his old dilapidated bike was a source of constant squabbles, as it had to be shared with his two brothers.

As Christmas approached, the two little boys discussed the possibility of Santa bringing them bicycles. Dick, who the year before had confirmed his suspicions of Santa Claus, discouraged them since he knew we couldn't afford any such expensive presents.

The boys woke before dawn on Christmas morning and tiptoed down to look under the tree. There, in shiny splendor, stood three bicycles. The youngsters were wild with joy as they examined their new treasures.

Dick looked closely at each name tag and with wide-eyed amazement said, "There REALLY is a Santa Claus. There really is." We have never regretted our decision that holiday season to spend an entire year's bonus to make three small boys' dreams come true, instead of spending it sensibly on necessities. Ten years later, the last two of our five sons are still riding two of those Christmas
BIKES. December 22, 1959

Almost Caught Him

Although it was many years ago, I have a memory of one particular Christmas that is as vivid as yesterday. We were a family with five small youngsters and could scarcely wait for Santa to arrive. He usually came to our house on Christmas Eve. Dad finally took us upstairs that we might see him arrive. We looked and looked, and then in the moonlight we could see a sleigh going down the road. Dad thought that it might have been Santa so down the stairs we rushed. Sure enough, when we opened the parlor door, the tree was lighted and the gifts were piled under it. Mother, sitting by the table mending, hadn't heard a sound.

That was the time we almost caught up with Santa.
THRILLED. December 20, 1941

Santa Quit Last Year

I'm interested to know how long Santa keeps coming to homes with children.

We always put out a little something extra for our two girls from "Santa," putting it either in their stockings, which hang from the fireplace mantel, or setting it on the hearth under the stockings. Last year, I suddenly realized they were 16 and 18 years old and still getting things from Santa. I decided it was slightly ridiculous and discontinued the custom.

Late Christmas Day, the girls were teasing me about not getting anything from Santa. The 16-year-old said when she came in and was whirling around in front of the fireplace she was also looking for something from Santa, though she really didn't think he would have left anything. Hope dies

HARD! December 25, 1979

Evidence Of Santa's Visit

Our son and his family were spending the holiday weekend with us. After the usual Christmas Eve festivities, the children had been tucked into bed. My daughter-in-law and I were busy in the kitchen, and the men were watching TV. The picture was quite fuzzy so our son volunteered to go out in the heavy snowfall to check the rooftop antenna mounted on the fireplace chimney. He remarked when he returned that the snowfall had ended.

After the excitement of opening the gifts on Christmas morning, the grandchildren bundled up and went outdoors to try out their new sleds. They ran to the top of the hill that overlooks our house.

Suddenly, Brad, 5, burst in the door shouting. "We saw Santa's footprints on the roof and they went straight to the chimney!"

Lisa, 9 years old and no longer a believer in Santa, added with a puzzled expression, "There really are tracks over to the fireplace chimney—come and see!"

We all walked up the hill to see Santa's footprints on our snowy

ROOFTOP. December 18, 1984

Santa Touches Noses

In order to get us children to go to sleep on Christmas Eve, Mother told us Santa would come into our bedrooms to check before he'd put any presents under the tree.

"How will Santa know we are asleep and not just faking?" we asked.

"Santa will touch your nose, and if you're really asleep, you won't feel it," was her reply.

Sure enough, on Christmas morning, each of us had a smudge of black soot on our noses where Santa had touched us. This is a tradition we still follow in our own
FAMILIES. December 3, 1985

Who Was That Mysterious Santa?

I heard the words Santa Claus for the first time because of this gift. I was not in school but was about ready to start—as soon as my sister was big enough to make the walk with me.

This particular Christmas morning, I remember seeing our next-door neighbor coming through the apple orchard between her house and ours. She was wearing a big apron, and we could see she had something in it.

She lost no time in telling my sister and me that Santa Claus had left something for us at her house the night before. The two toys were horses on rollers, something like those made from paper-mâché now. They were white with black spots.

"Santa Claus just made a mistake and left the gifts at the wrong house," she said.

As well as I can remember that was our very first toy. But who was Santa Claus? How did he know about two little girls? How did he get so near our home and still leave our gifts with a neighbor? All was a mystery. Santa Claus must be someone really wonderful.

The memory of that Christmas morning left more than a toy in my heart. When I recall the occasion, my eyes fill with tears, and I long for someone who has been gone for a long
TIME. December 12, 1978

Santa Gets Hug And Kiss

A few days ago, I was in a large store where all the Christmas things were on display. In one row there were three Santas—not alive—standing there. A woman and her tiny son came by. She walked right past, but the tiny boy walked up to one Santa and hugged and kissed him, then ran to catch his mother. Mother hadn't noticed what he had done. Oh, for the joy of tiny
CHILDREN. December 3, 1985

Slender Santa

Last year before Christmas, my friend took her 4-year-old, Teddy, shopping. There he saw the usual "what's up front that counts" Santa Claus.

Christmas Eve, Teddy's slim daddy in a Santa suit minus pillow burst into the living room with a jolly "Ho! Ho!" He rang his bells and handed out presents.

Teddy, big-eyed but skeptical, gravely accepted his many gifts. Finally he whispered, "Mommy, Santa got awful skinny since we
SAW HIM!" December 19-26, 1961

Santa Was Late In Arriving One Year

On Christmas Eve in 1925, Santa Claus almost forgot to come to our house. I was 5 years old with one little sister and two brothers. Our parents tucked us in early, reminding us to be good and go to sleep because jolly old Santa would be arriving soon. We had hung up our stockings, and the Christmas tree was trimmed and waiting. We even left a teacup and a piece of Christmas cake for Santa. We were filled with excitement but finally slept.

I was the first to get up Christmas morning. It was just daylight, so I awakened the other children and we tiptoed down to the parlor. To our surprise, there were no gifts. Our stockings were empty on the mantel over the fireplace. We all began to cry. Our father came running, followed by the family doctor and Mrs. Turner, our next-door neighbor. Papa said, "Stop all the crying. I have a surprise for you. We have a new baby girl. Come into Mama's room and you can see her."

We did as told and admired the newest family addition.

"Mama," said my oldest brother, "Santa Claus must have forgotten us. He didn't bring us anything and his cake is still waiting."

After the grownups had a conference, Mrs. Turner took us to her house for breakfast. "Don't worry about Santa Claus," she said, "he is late sometimes, but he always comes."

Sure enough, when we got back to our house there were presents for everyone under the tree. Our stockings were filled, and there was even a tiny stocking for the new baby.

When we were much older, we found out that our nice neighbor was the local midwife. Of course on that Christmas Eve, she, the doctor and my parents were much too busy to remember Santa
CLAUS. December 23, 1986

Admires A Stuffed Santa In A Window

The happiest collection at our house is my Santa collection. (Very few Santas are ever seen frowning.) About 10 years ago I admired a stuffed Santa holding a small Coke bottle in the window of an antique store. My husband bought him for $10. Later we realized it was a genuine Coke advertisement. It would be a miracle to find one at that price today.

That same Christmas, one of the girls gave me the cutest, fattest, Santa-shaped candle. I do not plan to ever light him. Another daughter made me a stuffed St. Nicholas pillow, and the third bought me a large ceramic Santa.

I have always loved Santa! I grew up in a time when kids believed in Santa longer than they do today. While I certainly respect the religious meaning of Christmas, I have never agreed with those who want to take Santa out of Christmas.

One can find old Santas at antique stores and flea markets. I found an unusual Santa bank at one for $6.50. I spotted an old Santa planter at another, but someone beat me to it. My Santa cookie jar came from an antique shop. Other old Santas include a

Santa candleholder, a Santa match box, and a paper-mâché Santa decoration from Holiday Inn (my daughter rescued him from the trash when she worked there). Unusual ones include a tiny kiddie Santa, a Santa made of burlap, a Santa who beats a drum when his battery is turned on, a Santa made of corn husks, Santa in a basket and a stained-glass Santa. In all, I have about 70 Santas and expect more this year.

I start getting my Santas out of the closet the Sunday after Thanksgiving. Most of the shelves in this closet are packed with Santas. I like to have time to enjoy them. I arrange them on the mantel, piano and lamp table in the living room and keep them out until Twelfth Night. Visitors enjoy seeing them. Santa is guaranteed to bring a

SMILE. December 4, 1984

I Remember Santa

My sister and I were fortunate children. Santa came to our house many times during the winter. Only once a year, however, did we see him. Always on Christmas Eve at dusk just before the lamps were lighted he came into our living room shouting "Merry Christmas." He patted our heads and said he was glad we had been such good little children and hoped we would enjoy our toys. Then he poured out the contents of his pack under our Christmas tree and left.

However, he came many other times to check on our behavior. Quite often he left a sack of candy in the empty bird nest that hung in the little tree outside our window. Mother often said how fortunate it was that we were playing happily instead of quarreling when Santa happened to look in. One morning two boxes of animal crackers hung over the dining room doorway, and once he left two coconuts at the front door.

But the most exciting time of all was when Daddy caught Santa. As we played upstairs we hear Daddy shouting excitedly, "Kids! Come quick! I've caught Santa Claus." We dashed for the stairs and rushed out the door.

"Why didn't you hurry?" Daddy said. "I couldn't hold him any longer, but I got these." He held three little red slippers trimmed with bunny-fur faces. The fourth lay on the ground where it had fallen during the scuffle. I was delighted, but little sister took hers soberly and asked Mother: "What if Daddy scared Santa away catching him like that? Maybe he won't come again."

But Mother smilingly assured her that Santa had had as much fun as Daddy and didn't scare that easily. And she was right; we had a lovely Christmas the next year.

ELLA. December 20, 1947

Yuletide Treats

Chapter 11

WHETHER IT WAS the fruitcake that mother began weeks ahead of time, or the luscious stuffing that Grandma made on Christmas morning from a recipe in her head, nearly everyone has a special food or drink that they associate with Christmas. The following letters do not contain recipes, but rather recollections of the foods and festivities that made the holidays special for readers.

So enjoy these letters filled with sugar and spice and everything nice. They're sure to make your mouth water for your favorite seasonal treat!

Egg-Coffee Aroma Filled The Chilled Air

Stories of past holidays abound this time of year. One of the most pleasant for me was gathering for a Swedish Christmas on a Midwest farm with my husband's family. They got together in good or bad weather, with a lighted tree, an armload of gifts and abundant good fellowship.

A special remembrance is his mother's delicious egg-coffee. Its fragrance filled the chill air long before we entered the house. Fresh-ground coffee, one good tablespoon per cup, was measured into a small bowl. A portion of slightly beaten egg, enough to moisten, plus a dash of salt, were stirred into the grounds. Already the fragrance was irresistible.

When the measured water began to boil in the coffeepot, the grounds with egg were carefully added, then allowed to simmer gently two or three minutes at the back of the stove. Sometimes only the egg white was used. A bit of the shell itself would make the coffee especially clear. A few tablespoons of cold water were added to settle the grounds. The use of a small sieve helped when pouring the coffee into cups.

If you, too, are expecting friends or family in for Christmas Eve—or anytime during the holidays—Grandma's delicious egg-coffee will be a pleasant

ADDITION. December 3, 1985

Jumbled Menu

Our Christmas dinner is always traditional; the menu is copied in a million homes. But Christmas Eve supper is something else.

For that meal each member of the family chooses one dish. It is a hilarious time, with much fun and laughter about the odd assortment of foods. This year, Bob has ordered oyster stew, Mary wants kraut and wieners, Grandma wants baked Idaho potatoes, Junior has asked for smoked herring and Dad requested white cake with seven-minute icing. And I am going to be—for the first time this year—free of all bread-making, for my order is simply for a loaf of

BAKER'S BREAD. December 18, 1956

Old Christmas Custom

We like to pull down the shades when we watch our Christmas pudding "burn." It is so simple and easy to do, and delights the children so that perhaps you will like to try it, too. In a large spoon place a cube of sugar. Over it pour lemon extract, almost filling the spoon. Hold the spoon over low heat (a match flame will do) to warm the extract, then touch the flame to the extract. Pour the burning extract over your pudding, slowly and carefully, and watch the kiddies' eyes sparkle.

SPIRIT OF YULETIDE. December 23, 1939

Christmas Pot-Luck

Cooperative dinners at Christmas do help the hostess a lot, providing they are well-planned in advance. But, oh, how they can backfire sometimes!

Last year we got word a couple of weeks before Christmas that a carload of my relatives would arrive for Christmas dinner. They live 60 miles from us, and my two married daughters and two daughters-in-law live close. The girls persuaded me just to bake the turkey and dressing and fix the dessert and coffee. Each of them would prepare a dish containing enough for the 28 who would eat together on Christmas.

About 10 o'clock the faraway guests arrived. About 11 Ellen and family arrived with a huge roaster of luscious baked beans.

Then came Henry and Alice, deep-bake dish in hand. They explained that they had just fixed beans because they thought the others would cook more Christmasy things. Then came Leon and family with—more beans.

When the last couple arrived we glanced toward their dish and asked, "Beans?"

"How in the world did you know?" they asked.

For dinner we had turkey, dressing, potatoes, pie and beans, beans and

BEANS! December 13, 1952

143

Cookies Exchanged

My wife came up with an ingenious method of baking a variety of Christmas cookies. She and nine of her friends made a list of the 10 most-desired cookies. The name of each cookie was placed in a hat and each of the women drew a name. About two weeks before Christmas each woman baked a big batch of the cookies she had picked. Then all the women exchanged cookies, taking some of each variety for the

HOLIDAYS. December 8, 1981

Santa's Refreshments

My parents brought 13 children into this world between 1913 and 1930, including three sets of twins. To say we were "hard up" at times is putting it mildly. In the '30s my father worked for $1 a day. Somehow my mother fed us and kept us in at least one change of clothing. She taught us to love God and respect the truth. She taught us that it is more blessed to give than to receive. At the time we were small; we didn't understand why, but we knew we had a glow inside us when we could share with someone more unfortunate, and believe me, in those days there were many.

My mother must have suffered those many Christmas seasons when Santa had to pass our house by on Christmas Eve. How she managed to make us know that Santa was poor, too, I'll never know. Even then we had a custom that means Christmas to us. Now we are scattered all over the United States, but I think we still have our "Santa's Cake" on Christmas Eve.

No matter how little we had, Mother always managed to have a beautiful snowy coconut cake to place on the table with coffee for Santa in case he did stop by our house. Even though we rushed from our beds and found no gifts in our stockings on Christmas morning, we always went to the kitchen first to see if Santa had had his cake. I can remember the happiness we felt when we saw one slice of cake missing, for we knew Santa had been there to see us and we had been able to share with him. This happiness carried us through the bitter disappointment of empty stockings with an understood promise that things would be better, and perhaps next year—who knew—our stockings might be bulging with gifts.

Now I put the Santa's cake on our kitchen table on Christmas Eve. I think of my mother giving her whole family a gift of love and unselfish devotion and a love of sharing that meant more than any trinket could have. I wish that everyone, especially children, could have a

SANTA'S CAKE. December 18, 1956

Old-Fashioned Menu Is Definitely Out

Today, with the temperature dropping and snow blowing, I began my Christmas menu and shopping lists.

The menu looked so much like last year's and maybe the year before that I wondered why I didn't do something different. How different? Well, down in my cookbook collection is Grandmother's *The Woman's Favorite Cookbook*. Maybe I'd have a real old-fashioned Christmas dinner. I started reading.

The Christmas menus began with breakfast. (Grandmother either had a staff of servants or never slept.) For breakfast she served oranges, broiled salt mackerel, chipped beef on toast, baked potatoes, griddle cakes, muffins and coffee.

For dinner, she served oysters on the half shell, cream of chicken soup, boiled whitefish with maître d'hôtel sauce, roast goose, applesauce, boiled potatoes, mashed turnips and sweet potatoes. This meal didn't end with store-bought ice cream. She served Christmas plum pudding, lemon ice, squash pie, quince jelly, Delicate Cake, salted almonds, fruit and coffee.

Then, would you believe, they ate supper! Having only cold roast goose, oyster patties, cold (not cole) slaw, Charlotte Russe, popovers and currant jelly.

Back to my menus, I guess we won't have an old-fashioned Christmas after all. And no one, not even Santa Claus, needs to expect an old-fashioned

BREAKFAST! December 9, 1986

Animal Cookies

Grandma started a Christmas tradition for us some 30 years ago. She rolled out a batch of sugar-cookie dough and cut out animals about six inches high—elephants, camels, lions and such—a pair of each. After baking, she frosted them white, and just before the icing set, pressed them into a pan of candy-coated caraway seeds.

The animal pairs were joined with toothpicks so they stood up. Side by side they marched, pair after pair, along a napkin-covered cardboard. There was only one pair of animals for each child, which made them seem more special.

Of course, we were charmed and never let Grandma forget our new tradition. Every Christmas the little folks in our family still ask for, and get, their

NOAH'S ARK COOKIES. December 18, 1956

Dad Dreams Up Christmas Salad Recipe

Nearly 20 years ago, when our children were babies, my husband decided he and the children would help me out by making the salad for our Christmas dinner. On Christmas Eve they all gathered around the kitchen table to make a whipped topping fruit salad he had dreamed up. For hours they sliced bananas, diced apples and chopped walnuts while discussing the possibility of Santa bringing everything they wanted.

When the next Christmas rolled around, the kids just assumed they were going to make "The Stuff" again. Before we knew it, we had a tradition. Over the years, the kids have added pineapple, raisins and coconut to the recipe. Dad stirs each contribution into his big mixing bowl while they chop, slice, dice and reflect upon Christmases past and future.

This tradition has become so important that when our daughter was considering which college to attend—one close or one far away—she was concerned whether she could get home for Christmas. Finally she said, "Don't worry, Dad, if I can't make it home for Christmas, I can still make The

STUFF." December 17, 1985

Cookie Party

What month could be more thrilling than December for a birthday? The holiday spirit fills the whole month. By the time my birthday comes, the last doll is dressed and the final toy animal is stuffed, and it's time to start Christmas baking.

In our family we traditionally have a cookie party on the weekend nearest my birthday. The recipe is an old one that's been used about 100 years that we know about. It makes five gallons of molasses ginger cookies. The dough is mixed the night before, and early the next day the children start rolling and cutting out the cookies. Baking goes on most of the day. The little children are guided to cut out a doggy, while the older ones take more responsibility, with the teenagers supervising the baking and decorating. The day closes with potato soup, ginger cookies, applesauce and a tired group of children looking forward to next year's cookie party on Grandma's

BIRTHDAY. December 6-13, 1966

Duff Was Special Treat For The Holiday

The crowning touch to our holiday dinners was Mother's Scottish Duff. Shortly before Christmas she assembled the ingredients for this special dish handed down from her Scottish grandmother.

Duff was a solid, sturdy concoction of dried bread crumbs, eggs, sugar, flour, spices and dried fruits. If times were lean, the fruit was simply raisins, but if more cash was available, Mother splurged by adding dried prunes or peaches. The sticky dough was tied up in a pudding bag and placed in a steam kettle, where it simmered for hours on the old wood range. The tantalizing odors had us begging for samples, even though we knew it was reserved for our Christmas feast. Mother served thick slices of duff swimming in rich vanilla or lemon sauce topped with whipped cream. It was truly a dessert for the gods.

I always pictured Great-Grandma's duff cooking in an iron pot over a smoke peat fire in her tiny cottage in Scotland. Now I can only dream about Mother's duff; she always made it from memory.

My husband thinks our holiday is incomplete if we don't have his Danish Mor's specialty, a tiny tidbit called *muesner*. The ingredients are simple, but baker's ammonia adds the magic touch that makes *muesner* unique.

Huge quantities of *muesner* were baked weeks before Christmas and stashed away in a pillowslip. Goodies had to be hidden from the five mischievous little children who would steal and devour the treats long before the holiday.

The children's childhood Christmas memories include those of dancing around the candle-lit tree as they sang the old carols in Danish. At last, they could eat all the *muesner* they
PLEASED. December 8, 1992

Company's Coming! So, Where's The Food?

My husband and I are long-haul truck drivers. Because we're gone from home so much, family get-togethers are all the more important. One year we agreed to have Christmas dinner at our house.

We were scheduled to get home in the late afternoon Christmas Eve. I figured I could stop by the grocery store on our way home from the truck company yard and pick up everything I needed to prepare the traditional dinner.

Even though the weather was bad and traffic was heavy, we managed to get to the grocery store by 6 p.m.—just in time to watch them lock the doors and head for home. I had forgotten that the store closed early on Christmas Eve!

Boy, was I in a fix! All of the relatives would be at our house the next day expecting a big dinner. Because we were seldom home, we didn't keep much food in the house. On Christmas Day, the family started arriving early. I explained my predicament to them, and we started looking through cupboards and the freezer to see what we could find.

We ended up with a very non-traditional, but delicious dinner of hot dogs, baked beans, potato salad and corn bread. But it didn't matter what we had to eat. It was the togetherness that
COUNTED. December 21, 1993

Christmas Pie Welcomed

My mother considered whipped cream pie absolutely for Christmas dinner.

We lived on a large farm, and there was always a big crock of heavy cream available. She had a special large pie pan in which she baked the usual crust and allowed it to cool. The cream was whipped to a thick consistency—sugar and flavoring added—then poured into the pie crust. On top was a smattering of chopped hickory nuts with dabs of colorful jelly. This was a rich dessert.

However, calories weren't in the limelight then, so everyone welcomed Mother's fattening, but so good, whipped cream
PIE. December 21, 1993

Everyone Enjoys Tradition But Mother

How was I to know that long ago when I made Monkey Bread, I was beginning a family Christmas tradition?

Our family has now grown to 26 members, and they all request their favorite food: Monkey Bread.

If they only knew how I hate to make it—I wonder if they would continue wanting it?

I begin by rolling those tiny balls of bread dough (I'm so glad I can buy frozen loaves now), dipping each in melted butter, rolling them in a mixture of cinnamon and sugar and placing them in two angel-food cake pans, letting them rise to double bulk, then pouring that delicious, gooey syrup of sugar, cinnamon and cream all over and sticking them in the oven.

It's always a treat when hubby helps dip the rolls in butter. We then have a good time reminiscing over the past 53 Christmases we've spent together.

The turkey with all the trimmings is always "second fiddle" to that darned Monkey Bread. Ah, well. Guess I'll keep on baking it. Have to keep the family
HAPPY! December 21, 1993

Just Not The Same If Menu Changes

Holidays just aren't holidays without our family's classic bread stuffing. It can be turkey or just plain chicken, as it was on the farm, but the bread stuffing with gravy has to be there.

The cranberry sauce: I remember mother working over stove and colander making it from fresh berries and straining out the skins. It would come out smooth and creamy, sweet and tart.

The pies were mincemeat and pumpkin. I don't especially like these, but the holidays would never be the same with any other kind. We switched to cherry later on, when Mother was no longer there to bake her specialties. Although we liked cherry better, it was never the same.

We have our own special item now—one that's too fattening— we don't fix it at any other time. It's a marinated sour-cream based fruit salad with marshmallows, which tastes as good as ambrosia. We all love it. Whatever is left over is split to go home with as many people as possible. That way no one gets too fat from one great

MEAL. December 8, 1992

Scratch Potatoes Better

Christmas dinner is not Christmas dinner in our house without mashed potatoes and gravy. Now, we've never had just those two items, but we couldn't have a Christmas meal without them. The potatoes and gravy must be made from scratch. There are all sorts of wonderful instant foods, but mashed potatoes and gravy are not among them.

Thanks to the miracle of the microwave, you can fix mashed potatoes early in the day or even the night before. Cover them tightly and refrigerate until needed. Heat in the microwave, stirring every three minutes. Add a little sweet or sour cream just before serving. You will have perfect potatoes without the last-minute

HASSLE. December 17, 1991

150

Noël Nostalgia

Chapter 12

W HAT DO YOU remember most about Christmas when you were growing up? Maybe you recall the year you got the little blonde-haired doll you had begged for from the Sears and Roebuck catalog. Maybe it was the year all the kids managed to make it home for the holidays. Perhaps it was the first melancholy Christmas spent without a loved one.

The following letters contain a potpourri of remembrances of Christmases past. The games, the gifts and the kind acts of others are all remembered in this scrapbook of Christmases gone by.

So Like A Mother

Christmas time always brings back memories to me of another Christmas, years ago. Mother and Father were alone in the old home, and being widely scattered and with many other interests, we had dropped the old habit of gathering at home for the day. Mother had been ailing, though we refused to consider it serious. We were all surprised, when some time before Christmas, we were invited to spend Christmas Day together at home. After she agreed to let us bring the dinner to spare her extra work, we gladly promised to come.

Christmas dawned, clear and cold, and a merry crowd met in the old home, with Mother the merriest of all. We were surprised to find a huge tree, beautifully decorated, with gifts for everyone— even the tiny great-granddaughter—all with the names written in Mother's clear, old-time writing. It was perfect, even to a jolly Santa Claus, and must have meant many weeks of work and planning.

It was months later that the sad realization was forced upon us that Mother would be leaving us before another Christmas came. Knowing that, she had planned for a last glad day together, well knowing how we would treasure the memory of it, though the joy be tinged with sadness.

DAUGHTER. December 24, 1932

One Small Boy's Gift Of Love

Christmas will soon be here again, and there is always a memory that is brought forth from my mind and relived each Christmas.

My son, John, was about 10 years old this particular Christmas—a bad time since my husband had been laid off from work and there were three other children to care for in addition to John.

John wanted so badly to get a present for his dad and me that he had taken his school lunch money for the week ($1.25) and saved it. While the rest of the children were enjoying their hot lunches, he would go out in the schoolyard so his teacher would think he'd gone home for lunch.

When Christmas was over he told me about this. He said, "Mom, I'd get so hungry. One day I found a candy bar on the play yard, and it sure tasted good."

On Christmas morning, there were two carefully wrapped packages under the tree—one for Mom and one for Dad. Both were from "Your son, John." Inside his dad's package were two cans of pipe tobacco and some cigarette papers.

Inside my package were two of the largest, glistening, blue stone clip earrings one could ever imagine. What if they were from the dime store? To me they were precious gems, and I wore them proudly, knowing the sacrifice John made to get them.

Today he is a husband and a father; I have to look up to that dear face instead of down to that happy little boy who, that beautiful Christmas morning, proudly reached for my present and said, "Here, Mom, this is for you from me."

I gave him life, but he has given so much more to me in his 21 years on this Earth. Is there any wonder that on that holy day, as I live over again the beautiful story of Jesus' birth, that I also go back and relive the story of a little boy's deep love and
DEVOTION? November 21, 1971

Christmas Party Game
A good ice-breaker to start off a Christmas party is "snowball." Divide the crowd into two sides. Line up the players and give each leader a basket decorated with holly and ribbons. On the floor before each line place a row of five cotton snowballs. The race is much after the fashion of a potato race. The first person picks up the snowballs, puts them in the basket and runs to deliver the basket to the next in line. This person replaces the snowballs on the floor in the proper place and brings the basket back to the next in line, who picks up the snowballs and puts them in the basket, delivering it to the fourth. This goes on until each player has run the course. A prize is given to the side that wins.
NEBRASKA. December 11, 1937

153

Santa Did The Sewing

The first Christmas I remember I was under 4 years of age. My sister and I both received big rag dolls, dressed alike. What was so special about this gift was that we thought Santa Claus had used Mama's sewing machine! The scraps, just like the dresses, were on the sewing machine Christmas morning.

Of course, Mama had sewn long into the night while we were asleep and was probably too tired to think about putting scraps away when she finished. I am so glad she didn't, for I still remember this very special Christmas of 65 years

AGO. December 12, 1978

Snow Was Too Deep For Santa

Many years ago this family lived on a little farm in North Dakota about 15 miles from Canada. The winters were very cold with lots of snow; they had a sod house with walls four feet thick. Where the three windows were set in the wall there was a sort of shelf almost two feet deep. A lamp sat on one of the shelves. Horses and cows were sheltered in a good barn for the winter. There was a fenced-in place for the chickens so the warmth from the other animals would keep them comfortable.

At the time this story begins, there were two girls; Lily and Lena, and three boys; Henry, Ed and baby Billy, who was only about 6 months old. He had been quite sick, and Mama had draped a sheet over the bed making a sort of tent. Under this she set a pan of hot water with medicine in it for Billy to breathe.

Though the children were small, they had to be told that Santa wouldn't be able to find them this year because the snow was so deep. It was over the windows, but the fact was the money had to go for food and Billy's medicine.

As Christmas came nearer, Daddy found a big tumbleweed lodged against the barn. He brought it into the house. The last time he had gone to town he brought cranberries home. Mama popped some corn and let the children string some of it along with a few of the berries. They decorated the tumbleweed tree and it made a bright spot of color on the little shelf. The little ones were so happy. On Christmas morning, after a good breakfast, they all gathered around Billy's crib. Daddy read from the Bible the story of the very first Christmas when baby Jesus was born in Bethlehem. Then they sang some songs Mama had taught them.

A very special treat came next. (Anything different in their simple lives was exciting.) Ever since the sheet had been over Billy's crib, the children had begged to be allowed to get under it to see what it was like to breathe the medicine. Little Brother was getting better fast, and since there were no presents, the children were permitted, one at a time, to crawl under the edge of the tent to inhale the vapors.

The dear lady who told this story to me said that of all the Christmases she has had, this is the one she remembers
BEST. December 12, 1978

Charley and Mortimer Visit Air Base Hospital

After attempting to have a quiet family gathering on Christmas Eve, 1952, the Edgar Bergen family changed their plans. This involved hectic late shopping, wrapping gifts, packing treats, other preparations and a rather long drive from San Francisco to Travis Air Force Base.

At Travis, they proceeded to the base hospital, the major entry point for military personnel returning from the Far East command for stateside medical care. The Bergens went directly to the ward for new arrivals from Korea and Japan.

The family was eventually able to convince the medical staff of their true identity, purpose, need for assistance and need for some medical carts. The family consisted of Mom, Dad, Candice, Charley McCarthy and Mortimer Snerd. After they were introduced, patients who were ambulatory quickly assembled, filling the ward. Much to the patients' delight Charley and Mortimer were successful in embarrassing the medical staff and the Bergens.

Eventually the family visited each patient, distributing gifts, snacks and chatting about home, family, girlfriends and experiences. Charley often inquired, "Man, what happened to you?" or "Buddy, you must like plaster." When asked about the visit to Travis, Edgar Bergen responded by saying, "We were enjoying a quiet evening at home and realized there were other things we must do on Christmas Eve."

I shall always remember the Bergen family with special fondness because I was one of the recipients with whom they shared the true Christmas spirit of

CARING. December 3, 1991

Most Exciting Christmas

I like to think of an exciting Christmas long ago when I was a little girl living on a farm in Kansas. The day before Christmas, our family—mother, father, my 8-year-old brother and I—drove to town to buy gifts and candy. It had snowed the day before and we were thrilled because we would have a white Christmas.

We hurried home that late afternoon. My brother and I ran around trying to help Mother with the supper and dishes, because there was to be a Christmas tree at the schoolhouse and Santa would be there. We'd never been taught there was a Santa Claus because my father didn't believe that way. Grandfather was a Methodist minister.

The parents of the neighborhood were going to go put their children's presents around the tree. My brother and I had seen our gifts, but we wanted to have our names called at the tree. So our parents took my wax doll with the golden curls and my brother's red-topped boots to the Christmas tree.

The little schoolhouse was crowded with farmers and their families, and the tree was a blaze of lights from tiny candles fastened on the branches. There were no electric lights. Popcorn strings twined among paper chains made by the pupils, and branches were heavy with cotton snow.

Everyone sat on the edge of his seat awaiting Santa. Up went a window, and jolly old Saint Nick clambered into the room. With him came a blast of icy wind.

156

Some of the candles on the tree were blown over, and in an instant the cotton-wrapped branches were blazing.

Pandemonium followed. The teacher fainted. Excited people rushed for the door—just one door! One woman threw her baby out of a window into the snow. Rescued immediately, it was unharmed. Another woman screamed, "Where's Eddie?"

When Eddie was located she stood screaming, "Where's Eddie's hat?" All the time the building blazed. It burned to the ground, taking all our Christmas toys with it. But nothing was hurt except the children's hearts—and a child's heart heals rapidly. We were taught to expect the best, prepare for the worst, and to accept without grumbling whatever

HAPPENS. December 20, 1952

So Happy That Day

The happiest Christmas I have ever known was the year I was 9 years old. Mother was in bed with a new little brother, so she couldn't get to town to get things for us older children. However, we were too small to realize that—you see, we still believed in Santa.

Dad never paid any attention to us children nor to Christmas giving. He would have been the last person we would ever have thought would try to keep Christmas for us.

But Christmas morning came and there were apples, candy, nuts and even an orange for each of us. Dad told me to look under the bed. There I found a lovely little doll in a box. She was dressed in a pink dress and cap.

Then Dad took us outside. There in the snow, propped against the kitchen, was the ladder Santa had used to climb up on the roof. Yes sir, there were his footprints—some apples, nuts and even an orange. We were three mighty happy kids that Christmas Day. Santa Claus did come! We had seen the proof.

As I grew older and realized how those things came to be there, my heart was filled with love for my dad for giving me the happiest Christmas I have ever had.

ONE WHO REMEMBERS. December 20, 1941

Mothers 'N' Christmas

I like to think of the Christmases my mother made for me. I have only to close my eyes to smell the popcorn and the never-forgotten scent of pine! I can see my mother's shining eyes, and the many little things she did to make the holidays happy ones for us all. With a pang, I remember how little she received compared to the rest of us. Today I can count the sacrifices our Christmases cost her.

Every year her father would send her a check, which she was supposed to spend on herself. But did she? Not much. The money was always used for the things the rest of us coveted.

I would not trade any material possession—not anything—for the memories my mother built for me so long ago. Just as Mary, mother of Jesus, was the one who suffered and gave that Christmas so many ages ago, mothers of today give for their children, suffering and sacrificing gladly. To every mother a God bless you and a

MERRY CHRISTMAS! December 7, 1935

Santa Forgot Dad

I remember, all too plainly, one Christmas when we forgot father. I spent cold hours in unheated rooms embroidering linens that were a surprise for mother. I racked my brain to think of unusual gifts for friends and cousins. I dropped hints for the things I especially wanted for myself.

Christmas day came and went. That evening a neighbor dropped in and during the conversation directed this question to Dad: "What did you get?"

He replied with a smile—it was a little sad. "Santa Claus forgot me this year."

With a start we realized that in our hustle and hurry we had forgotten dear old Dad. After the guest had departed, Mother and I scolded him for embarrassing us before company.

He is gone from this world now, and I would give up much if I might have the privilege of buying a gift for him this Christmas.

ZENOBIA. December 16, 1939

Weevils Destroy Santa's Cotton Crop

When I was young we lived in the Ozark Mountains on a small farm. My father farmed with a team of horses; tractors were unheard of then.

All the money we had was from a few eggs and a bucket of cream each week until we picked the cotton in the fall. Then we would buy clothes, new blankets and anything we just had to have.

One fall when I was about 8 years old, my mother told me, my younger brother and sister that Santa wouldn't visit us that year because the boll weevils had destroyed his cotton crop and he wouldn't have money for toys.

Mother told me later that the thought of us having absolutely nothing for Christmas was too much for her. She took an old sheet and made pillowcases about 6 inches by 12 inches, dyed them red and filled them with sugar cookies. Some were round, some square, some three-cornered, and some were long strips.

Those were the best cookies I had ever eaten. I'm 74 now, and many gifts have come my way, but none ever as nice as those sugar cookies on Christmas
MORNING. December 17, 1985

This Grandpa Always Loved Christmas

My husband's father didn't have the best of health during the last few years of his life, but as our four children (two girls and two boys) always said, "Grandpa loved Christmas."

Grandpa lived on the farm and didn't leave home often. The one thing he did like to do was come to our house the day before Christmas and spend the night and Christmas day watching the children in all their excitement.

In those last few years Grandma would say, "I'm sure we just can't make it this year, Papa isn't so well." However, on December 24, I'd receive a call saying, "I guess Papa feels better, we'll be over pretty soon." About three in the afternoon, there they were.

We'd all eat with lots of excitement, then drive to the church for

159

the Christmas Eve program. Then we would go back home for cookies and drinks. Every bed was full. The boys were on a roll-out bed because they had given their bed to grandparents.

Early the next morning, there was news of Santa's visit with gifts and candy. Then came breakfast, the arrival of other relatives, an exchange of gifts and lots of chatter. After a short nap for Grandpa, we were ready for a noon Christmas dinner of turkey and all the trimmings. As the smiling grandparents left for home late Christmas day we realized they had gained a little out of life.

As I stop to think, my husband and I are now Grandpa's

AGE. December 4, 1984

Tragedy Of Long Ago

It's been seventy years or more Kate, since that long-ago Christmas when I got the doll from Santa Claus. Although I was about 8 or 10 years old, it was the first one I had ever had, and I was in seventh heaven. I loved that doll so that I took her to bed with me.

The day after Christmas was a sad one for me, because during the night I laid on my lovely dolly and somehow the head came loose from the body. How I cried! My mother soothed me, got her needle and thread and fastened the head back on. But part of the magic spell was broken, for my parents had told me not to take the doll to bed with me, and though mended, she was never quite the same again.

SAD ALICE. December 23, 1944

Dad Watched For Santa

The thing I remember about Christmas at our house was how early we opened our gifts on Christmas morning.

If my sister or I did not waken early enough, my father would awaken us—at 3 or 4 a.m. He couldn't

WAIT! December 21, 1993

160

Scout Troop Adopts Prisoners For Christmas

When I was a scoutmaster, our troop decided to adopt some inmates at a nearby prison as a Christmas project. After some reflection, the prison superintendent selected 12 prisoners who seldom received mail and wouldn't expect any contact from relatives at Christmas.

Three evenings before Christmas, we went to meet them. The noise level among the boys lowered perceptibly as we entered the prison parking lot. It was dark, so the spotlights and guns in the towers were clearly visible. The guard captain met us at the gate. After everyone signed in, the gate closed with a resounding clang, long remembered by every member of our party. We were escorted to the dining hall in single file, with no one speaking on the way.

The prisoners walked in slowly and shyly. They ranged from the early 20s to grizzled old-timers. Our visit lasted about 45 minutes. One scout had brought a guitar, and the ice was broken somewhat as he played carols. Soon the boys, guards and prisoners were adding their voices to the third and fourth songs. One scout distributed a box of cookies his mother had baked, and the boys met individually with prisoners whom they had been assigned. Although conversation didn't come easily, I was proud of the boys for their interest and skillful avoidance of embarrassing questions and comments. There were more than a few tears visible in the eyes of the prisoners, and the scouts—normally a boisterous lot— were quiet and deeply moved.

When the guard indicated our time was nearly up, we all joined in singing "Silent Night." Never have I seen a group so affected by this. When it ended, a gray-haired prisoner stepped forward and thanked us on behalf of the group. He added a simple, firmly expressed, "God bless you."

After we again heard the clang of the gate, we reflected on how it would feel to be unable to shop for a gift or Christmas card for anyone and be unable to see the bustle in the streets and hear "Merry Christmas" spoken

EVERYWHERE. December 4, 1984

Mistletoe Memories

There's something about mistletoe that makes me feel quivery all over. Just to see bits of it in the windows under the lights, makes me feel 16 again instead of 40. Mistletoe brings back old memories and girlhood dreams. I wonder if I dare put up some this year, when I catch all of them out of the house. Would the family guess I'd put it there? They would! And they'd rib me a plenty. Because to them I am just a sentimental

OLD SUSAN. December 18, 1937

Bessie Delivers On Christmas Eve

"Here it is Christmas Eve! It's cold and dark and Bessie picks this time to calve," my father exclaimed as he pulled out two well-used old lanterns to fill with kerosene. My mother bundled us up, and we warmed ourselves near the fireplace that already had the all-night log burning. We glanced at the long, empty stockings that hung on the mantel. There was a bit of sadness on our faces, but not for long, as our dad knew how to reassure us.

"Santa Claus understands better than we do about cows calving on Christmas Eve. We don't have to worry about him skipping you because you aren't in bed.

"She's probably in that large clump of pines over on the hill where she's found lots of pine straw," said our daddy as we went out single file toward the cold-looking trees. My father led the way, carrying a lantern in one hand and my younger brother over a shoulder with the other. Mother brought up the rear with my other brother and me in-between, fully protected.

It was truly a miracle watching old Bessie give birth to a new calf. How exciting to watch my dad and Bessie bathe and handle the new little long-legged baby!

Then my dad turned to my mother, and with a twinkle in his eye said, "Katie, the children and I will take care of Bessie and her baby. Some hot chocolate would taste good when we get to the house. Why don't you go on and take care of that chore while we bed old Bessie down in the stable?"

It was so satisfying to think we had a part in helping Bessie and her baby calf back to the barn and into one of the stables where we bedded them down for the night.

There were more surprises when we entered the warm house. No long, limp stockings greeted us from the mantel. Instead, there were fat ones bulging with goodies from good old Santa Claus.

We never asked if my mother encountered Santa, but the usual piece of cake was gone from the dining room

TABLE. December 20, 1983

Shops At Dime Store

The first Christmas presents our son bought for his father and me were purchased at the dime store. He was about 7 years old, and I was impressed by his practical good sense. It was during the Depression, and his allowance was meager. He went alone to the store and spent the large sum of 10 cents on each of us.

On Christmas morning he proudly presented his father with two cakes of shaving soap and gave me a package of hairpins. His gifts have stayed in my mind for almost 50

YEARS. December 8, 1981

German Dad Could Make Anything From Tin

My most memorable Christmas tree was made by the loving hands of my dear father, who was born in Germany and came to America when he was 18. An expert tinner, he learned his profession after living in Newark, New Jersey, for a few years. He then came to Kansas with his wife and three children. I was the youngest.

He established his tin shop in Newton. Money was scarce in those days. We were poor, but didn't know it, because we were happy with what we had. In those days, many utensils were made of tin. Dad made everything from wash boilers to coffeepots.

Since we couldn't afford a Christmas tree, he made a tin one. It was three to four feet tall. The main stem was a tin pipe. Soldered to it were many wavy branches with hundreds of holes to tie on decorations. A coat of pretty green paint gave it a good appearance. At the top was a basket formation to be filled with fruit. On each branch was a candleholder.

Mother made cookies for the tree using forms made by my father. There were cookie birds, rabbits, fiddles, dolls, dogs, horses and boots on the tree. We also painted English walnuts with gold and silver to hang on the tree. Each year we enjoyed stripping the tree after the holidays and eating the goodies. The tree was then carefully folded and put in the attic.

The year finally came when we discarded the tin tree and enjoyed a real one. We felt no one would want a tin tree, so it was crushed and put in the trash. That was a mistake, for I often wish I had it. I'm now 92 years of age and blessed in so many
WAYS. December 16, 1975

Christmas On A Claim

Many years ago, when Oklahoma was very young, times were hard. In order to pull through, many menfolk left the women and children to hold the fort while they went back to the "states" to get jobs to tide them over until the next crop season.

Dad went back to Kansas to work, and Mother and I and my four younger brothers and sisters were left to take care of things. The days on the lonely claim were long, and the nights seemed even longer as we listened to the eerie cry of an owl or the weird howl of a nearby wolf.

Now and then a band of Indians stopped to beg food or water. Once when Mother told them she barely had enough food for her own family, a big, burly Indian pushed past her and calmly helped himself to a sack of cornmeal. Mother was too frightened to protest.

We began wondering what we would do for Christmas with so little. The day before Christmas, Mother sent the four younger children to gather little red skunk berries to decorate our cabin. Then she dragged out our last can of sorghum molasses and made taffy.

That night all of the children fell into bed happy except me. I was

164

older, and I realized the Christmas ahead was unlike any I had known. Long after the other children were asleep, I lay awake, wishing that something would happen to change our dull, unhappy Christmas into a bright one like those I remembered. Eventually I fell asleep.

In the middle of the night I awakened by the sound of hushed voices. When I squinted through the lamplight that softly bathed the room, there stood Father! He and Mother were unpacking a big box of things he had brought back from the "states." Boxes, sacks and bright packages lay on the chairs and the floor. It was like a glorious dream come true, as if Santa himself had

ARRIVED. December 20, 1955

How We Do Enjoy It

My greatest Christmas surprise came two years ago, when our nine children put their savings together and installed a new radio in our country home while we were attending a Christmas tree celebration at the church. When we returned, the children were seated around the room listening to a Christmas program from Los Angeles. Now, after two years, with the children all away from home, we feel it almost brings them to us as we listen to the various programs over the air. No surprise could have given Father and me more pleasure.

A MOTHER. December 19, 1931

The Elusive Cranberries

This is an interesting game for the Christmas party. There are two couples at each table, both interested in spearing more cranberries with their joint hatpin than the other couple is able to spear. Each couple is instructed that they must both hold the same hatpin, using only one hand. The cranberries, as speared, naturally are forced up the hatpin. The couple having the longest line of berries on its hatpin wins.

MRS. WILL UMPHRES. December 12, 1931

No Shortage Of Spirit

Odd things sometimes happen when people are short on cash. My brother Bill chuckles whenever he recalls how his family kept face with ours one particular Christmas during the Depression.

They were living in Arizona, and we were living in Kansas. I decided to send money to his family since I had no idea what they really needed. So, I enclosed a $5 bill in a Christmas card and sent it on its way. I wished that it was a crinkly new bill, but I reasoned that an old one was worth just as much.

The day before Christmas a card came from Bill's family. It said that since they couldn't know what we needed the most, they had decided to send money. Enclosed in the card was a crisp new $5 bill. They didn't mention receiving our card, so I supposed that the cards had passed in the mail. Times were so hard then that I was delighted to see money for a gift.

Ten years later Bill came back to our home for a visit. As we were both fairly prosperous once again, Bill laughed and told me the real story of my Christmas gift. When my Christmas card to them arrived, they were down to the barest existence and knew they could never send a gift. So, while his wife addressed a Christmas card, he ran out and exchanged my old bill for a brand-new one, enclosed it in the envelope and mailed it to me. He said it was the hardest thing he had ever done, for he so needed the money. Yet his pride would not allow him to accept when he was unable to give.

We had a good laugh as I remarked that we both had gotten off that year with a card and a 3-cent
STAMP. December 22, 1953

He Brings Happiness

When I was 9 years old, Mother became ill and was in the hospital for several weeks. I was an only child, and my daddy cared for me and the farm during the bad winter of 1948. It was a pretty lonely time, and Christmas was coming soon.

My little rural school was planning a Christmas program. I

looked a mess. My hair was long, straight and tangled. Daddy would become so exasperated trying to brush it, he'd reach for the scissors and cut out the knots. Imagine!

Before our program, he took me to town for a haircut and my first permanent. He then bought me a rust-colored taffeta dress. It had a ruffle in a darker shade around the bottom of a full gathered skirt. It had a big sash in the back and little puffed sleeves. I loved the way it rustled when I moved. I felt like a princess.

I'll never forget that dress. And I still love that daddy who, though busy and worried, cared enough to make a little girl
HAPPY. December 3-10, 1974

Couldn't Cry After That

The turkey just wouldn't stay trussed up gracefully, like Grandmother's turkeys always did. Dressing oozed out his neck, and he wasn't nice and golden brown at all. The pumpkin pies didn't look like they were going to "set" properly. The Christmas cookies scorched while I was trying to remember how much sugar to put in the cranberry jell—and then the crowning touch—the pudding sauce boiled over into sizzling lakes on my cookstove.

I scraped up the mess. The heat from the stove combined with the blush of shame at my cooking ignorance to make my face beet red. I bitterly regretted ever promising to cook our first Christmas dinner together—Jack's and mine—with my own inexperienced hands. I could at least have picked out something easy to fix.

Then Jack came in. He didn't notice the mess at all, or that I was close to tears. He just kissed me and said: "Gee, you look pretty with your cheeks so pink like that. M-mm, that turkey smells good!" And when he thought I wasn't looking, he sneaked a cookie and ate it as if it were the best cookie ever made.

Well, in spite of everything you may be sure I perked up and made a success of that dinner. We laugh at that first Christmas dinner now, but Jack is still just as kind and loving as he was then, though it's nearly 20 years now that I've been
MRS. JACK. December 25, 1937

An Old Man's Gift

The windows were ablaze with toys and attractive gifts, surrounded with tinsel, cotton and holly. Christmas shoppers thronged the streets, their faces pink from the cold December air, flushed with the eagerness and spirit of the season. Here and there tiny snowflakes whirred hesitantly from a gray, half-promising sky.

Two small newsboys stood staring hungrily through the artistically draped window at a miniature airplane, posed realistically in the air. Two chapped red hands clutched a half-dozen papers, and two small pinched faces bore the unmistakable signs of poverty and undernourishment. In the hurrying, scurrying crowd, no one took time to notice the covetous looks on those two small boys' faces.

Presently an old man, stooped with age and cruelly bent with rheumatism, paused and glanced down at the urchins, who stared back at him, half-impudently, half-apologetically. "Come Chet, we gotta hurry," said the older.

"Hello boys," quavered the old man. "Like that airplane? Some contraption, eh? Like to have that for Christmas, I bet you would. Pshaw! Let me see..." He fumbled anxiously in his pockets.

"Sure we would," grinned the boys, "but no danger of us getting anything like that this year—gee, ain't it keen? I wish Ma wussn't sick, and Dad had a job like he used to have. Nope, Dad hasn't worked for two years. Chet and me'll probably have to go down on the tracks and pick up coal Christmas Day."

"Here lads, take this." The old man placed a bill into the eager palms. "Go in and buy that airplane—take the change home to your mother and tell her to buy the biggest turkey and all the fixin's your Dad can find. And you boys stay off the tracks Christmas Day, see?"

The old man turned roughly away, an unshed tear trembling in his dim old eyes while he fumbled feebly for a last $10 bill.

Mrs. B.H. December 20, 1941

"What Big Eyes You Have"

Were the Christmas trees of my childhood really so tall and wonderful? Seems to me their tips swept the ceiling. The branches were loaded with dolls and toys, while beneath were huge piles of mysterious-looking bundles. I tell my children about the Christmas trees of my childhood. They listen eagerly, if a little doubtful. I see a knowing wink between them. They have visited some of the places I knew in my childhood and found them greatly lacking in the wonderment I had pictured. Had these scenes actually deteriorated, or was it that my modern youngsters have seen so much more? Or was it, as they secretly believe, that Mother imagines things?

ADDIE MAY. December 11, 1937

Christmas Blessings Were Shared With Tramp

My mother was 17 years old in 1893, the year a severe depression hit the nation. Her father was a poor dirt farmer in a frontier community in western Iowa. Some of his land was still unfenced native grassland. The nearest town was 14 miles away. This is a story Mom told frequently in the last years of her life. She lived to be 96. This was translated from her Low German.

"It was Christmas Eve, 1893. There were no presents for us children, and no decorated evergreen tree stood in our front room (we called it the parlor), but we were happy. We enjoyed the blessings of family togetherness, something no money can buy.

"All day long my two younger sisters and I helped Mama prepare supper. Our supper on Christmas Eve was our biggest meal of the year, in honor of the most holy of nights.

"By suppertime our kitchen table was loaded down with good things to eat: a large German blood pudding with plum sauce, a fat roast goose, apple and sage dressing, plenty of boiled potatoes, rich brown gravy, fresh black bread, coffee cake and two big custard pies. Only a few staples were purchased in town. The rest my parents raised.

"Just before we sat down to say grace and share the bountiful blessings of food, we heard a soft knock at the kitchen door. 'Who can that be?' Papa wondered. It was a bitterly cold night, and the snow was deep.

"As Papa opened the door, we saw a tramp. He was a small man, old and frail. He seemed very cold, though he was dressed warmly in good, thick clothing.

"Papa drew the tramp into our cozy kitchen and invited him to the table. My, how hungry he was! How he ate! As the food was passed, dish after dish, he would say with deep humility, 'Thank you. Thank you. Oh, you are so kind.' Like us, he spoke Low German.

"When the meal was over, the tramp asked permission to spend the night in the hayloft of our barn. Papa was a man of great compassion and refused to hear of this. He said no guest of his would sleep outdoors. There was a problem. We had no spare bed and no extra quilts or blankets. Then our hired man volunteered to sleep with the tramp.

"The tramp had breakfast with us the next morning, then left. We often wondered where he went, where he ate his next meal, and what became of him.

"There were no government programs for the poor in those times. The poor had to survive on their own the best they could," Mom

FINISHED. December 6, 1983

Tricycle Was An Impossible Dream

The year was 1932, and I was 3 years old. My parents wanted to get me a tricycle for Christmas, but it had been a drought summer, and the Great Depression gripped the land. They had bought a small farm and hoped to be able to survive, but it was looking more doubtful all the time. The idea of an expensive $2.95 tricycle seemed like an impossible dream.

A neighbor man gave Daddy $1 to take him to town to do a little shopping. Maybe they had a bit more money, but it was certainly not enough to do very much shopping for the family. They knew they must forget the trike.

It was a cold, rainy night. Daddy's car was a coupe, so the neighbor man crowded into the seat with Mother and Daddy. I sat on Mother's lap. As we rounded a curve in the highway, still several miles from town, our headlights shone on an overturned car in a deep ditch. A man was standing on the road waving a white cloth as rain beat down on him. Back then, you could feel safe helping someone in distress, so Daddy stopped.

A family from New York, coming to our city in Missouri for Christmas, had skidded on the rain-slick curve. The daughter was injured. The men formed a rescue chain and lifted the girl and her mother out of the wrecked car. The two of them crowded into our car, and I remember they bound the girl's bleeding knee with Daddy's handkerchief. The man and our neighbor rode the rest of the way in the rumble seat, hunkering close to the back glass of the car to keep as dry as possible.

Daddy took the people to their folks' house, and the man insisted on giving him $5. He appreciated our help at such a critical time.

Guess what I got under the tree on Christmas morning! I rode that tricycle a million miles, until finally the wheels just wobbled off and couldn't be repaired any more.

"Do unto others as you would have them do unto you" paid off then, and it is still a good practice
TODAY! December 9, 1986

Virginia Party Was Enjoyed By All

Last year a woman in our town finally fulfilled a dream to have a "Virginia Party." Of course, the inspiration for the party was the well-known and well-loved letter to a little girl who wrote to her local newspaper to find out if there really was a Santa Claus. We all know the reply: "Yes, Virginia, there is a Santa Claus." The story has become a classic.

Through the monumental efforts of this Virginia, a party was enjoyed by over 30 Virginias in our area. Phone calls were the spark, and by placing notices in local papers she contacted as many Virginias as she was able. Harry, her husband, produced an early Christmas present in the form of a movie camera that would produce film to be viewed through TV.

Guests were filmed as they arrived, and we will get to see the film at the party this year. Lovely buffets were set up in both the dining room and recreation room. Each guest received a gift and a copy of the Virginia story.

Some of us were acquainted already, but we made new friends because of this lovely dream of our hostess. Virginia is no longer a name given to girl babies, so most of us were older. However, we were delighted to have a teenager among the guests.

This was really a fun idea. Those who were lucky enough to attend the first Virginia party are looking forward to another with
ENTHUSIASM! December 18, 1984

Santa's Wonderful Miracles Began To Happen

Father had had surgery, so sister and I knew there would be no Christmas tree on which to hang ornaments, popcorn or cranberries. Mama (my grandmother) lived in another city. Her coming at Christmas meant almost as much as Santa. On this particular Christmas, ice and snow kept the trains from running. She telephoned and said, "When you can't change a situation, smile and look for the good in it." We didn't see anything good in Mama not coming.

No Santa, no presents, no tree, no Christmas food, no Mama— and Father sick in bed. As I helped sister carry in wood from the snow-covered pile, hot salty tears trickled down my face. Christmas Eve and no Santa—it wasn't fair!

Darkness fell on the white snow; lights began glimmering in windows of the farmhouses. Suddenly we saw an automobile slowly making its way through the ruts. It was turning in at our house. Who could be coming? A little white-haired, sweet-faced woman got out, and the man handed her a big bag. Mama! We ran to hug her.

"Today was the first time the trains ran," she told us. In a jiffy, she had her apron on and was baking Christmas cookies, spicy mincemeat pies and a coconut cake.

Suddenly there was heavy knocking at the door. There stood two neighbors with a huge cedar Christmas tree. "Knew you wouldn't have a tree and we wanted to be Santa." They put it up, and it reached the ceiling. The entire room was filled with delicious cedar aroma.

Mama said, "One of my neighbors gave me some hand-painted ornaments from Germany, and I brought them to you." She unwrapped a big box, and we decorated the tree.

One of Mama's favorite songs was "Be not dismayed what'er betide, God will take care of you." I thought of her song as I looked at our family. I knew Santa's greatest gifts in the world were in front of

ME. December 18, 1984

Beth's "I Love You"

The most wonderful Christmas gift I have ever received was perhaps a queer one to others, for it was the gift of "I love you," from my 6-year-old Beth. How strange that must seem to others who hear such childish words often.

My baby was taken from me when she was but an infant. I was in poor health and had to travel to regain it. For five years I was a stranger to baby Beth. Then finally she was allowed to live with us, and I began anew, as her mother. She used to cry for hours for her grandmother, who had cared for her during my absence. It was on Christmas morning, when overjoyed by the many gifts Santa had left, that she rushed to me and threw her arms about me, crying, "Momee, I love you." What mother could wish for more? To me, it was better than all other gifts.

MRS. W. December 19, 1931

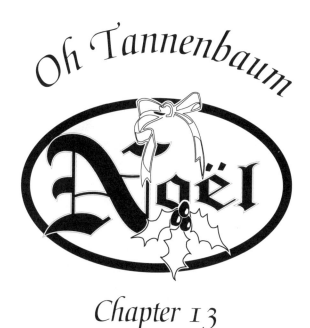

Oh Tannenbaum

Chapter 13

ONE OF THE best-loved holiday festivities in America is finding and decorating the Christmas tree. The modern tree—a combination of Roman, German, and other early European civilizations' traditions—dates back to 1605. These early trees were decorated primarily with edible ornaments, such as nuts, cookies and marzipan. In those days, children were more excited about taking the tree down than putting it up, for when the tree was dismantled the goodies were theirs.

Almost 400 years later, the Christmas tree still brings joy to young and old alike. The following are readers' stories of their most memorable trees.

Christmas Tree Farewell

Here it is, getting close to the time when you must say "farewell" to your Christmas tree. It seems that most people take their trees down the day after New Year's. In some ways this is a sad time, for it means the end of the holidays, which are always so much fun for everyone. Why not have an "Un-Trim-the Tree" party? This can be either for your family or friends. Have a lettered box for each kind of tree trimming so that everyone will know where things go. You might give a small candy prize to the people who get their share of the trimmings off without breaking any. If you make a party of this, you may want to leave the tree inside until the next morning. This is a good time to talk over the holiday SEASON. December 29, 1953

Holly Tree Is Decorated By Nature

I was born in 1931. My mother died when I was a few days old, and I was taken to live with my maternal grandparents on a run-down farm. Grandpa was not able to work away from home. Grandma traded eggs for sugar, flour, salt and bare necessities. They grew the rest of our food.

Christmas was especially happy for me because I always got some candy, apples, oranges and a gift or two, but we never had a tree. When I started school, the other girls talked for days about decorating their Christmas trees.

When I was 9, I told Grandma I wanted a tree to decorate. She patiently explained that we didn't have any money for trimmings, and we didn't have any popcorn. I told my grandpa, who was my best friend in all the world, that I wanted a tree. One day when I came home, Grandpa had a smile on his face, and his gray eyes twinkled. "There's a surprise for you in the bedroom," he said.

What joy and happiness when I saw a holly tree covered with shiny red berries, a tree decorated by nature! I realize now Grandpa must have spent many hours walking through the woods hunting the right tree.

More than 40 years have passed, and I still have a special

feeling about Christmas trees. I hang each beautiful ornament with care. When the tree is finished I turn on the lights and stand back to enjoy the beautiful creation. I always go back in memory to the holly tree. Grandpa's love was not bound by poverty; he found a way to bring happiness to a little girl's

HEART. December 22, 1987

First Christmas Tree

We'd been married six months, and it was Christmas Eve. We had to have a Christmas tree.

In this particular Southern state where my husband was working, pine trees grew tall and prolific in forests, even near the shoulders of the road.

My husband cut down one of the smaller trees that reached to our ceiling.

We were in a hamlet that sold no baubles to put on the tree, so I cut out Christmas objects from a catalog and magazine and pasted them on cardboard cut to the size and design of the pictures. I glittered them and used an ice pick to make a hole for a ribbon to go through so they could hang on the tree. The homemade objects were colorful and sparkled. It was fun creating them.

To me, it was the most beautiful tree I ever had in our 42 years of

MARRIAGE. December 22, 1992

"Christmas Past" Trees

We select a nicely shaped evergreen tree from a reliable nursery each Christmas season. On an agreed date the tree arrives packed in soil with burlap. We place it in a tub and add water to it from time to time to keep it fresh. We have a lovely Christmas tree for indoors, and in about 10 days we plant it in our front yard.

We now have four beautiful trees from previous years. It's a grand way to add beauty to your yard at so little

EXTRA COST. December 10, 1949

No Tree Will Ever Compare

Our Christmas tree of 1934 will live forever in my memory. Those were Depression days. A married brother, his wife and baby had moved into our large house to save on expenses. There were seven of us then, and only my brother had work on a farm at 50 cents a day. It was a major struggle to keep food on the table, so my brother often supplemented the menu by bringing home a rabbit he had shot while walking home from work.

Christmas came, and all of us had to use our ingenuity to make gifts for one another. Mother was the most ingenious though, for she sent my sister and me out to bring in the largest tumbleweed we could find. Then Mother made a sticky syrup and poured it over the tumbleweed, sprinkling on artificial snow as she poured. How it did glisten! After it was dry, Dad planted it in a pail of dirt. Then we carefully decorated the weed with colored rope and the lightest and daintiest of our decorations, so the branches would not break. We covered the pail with last year's Christmas wrap, while Mother dressed a small celluloid doll as an angel for the top of our tree. I can still visualize the gossamer wings, the tinseled halo and trim.

Our homemade gifts and gift wrappings that year were unique and quite clever, but nothing before or since has ever quite topped the wonderful, sparkling tumbleweed Christmas tree, so literally
PRICELESS. December 31, 1970

Practical Joke Grew

A few weeks before Christmas my father called me and said, "If you haven't got your Christmas tree yet, come on out. I have found the perfect tree for you."

My husband took me out to Father's house in the country.

When I got there my father showed me a tiny cedar tree, about one inch in height. He had transplanted the tree into a flat pound coffee can. Going along with my father's sense of humor, I accepted the tiny tree in the spirit in which it was given.

Taking the tree home, I tended it carefully, changing it from smaller flowerpots to larger containers as needed.

Then came the day when my tree was set outside in our front yard. It grew rapidly into a 14-foot, beautifully shaped tree. What had started as a practical joke had turned into an object of beauty for me. For many years my tree blossomed with colored lights and tinsel during the Christmas

SEASON. December 3, 1991

German Christmas Tree Has Interesting History

This year, my Christmas tree is 64 years old, the same age as me. I was born January 17, 1922, in Akron, Ohio. In December of that year Santa Claus brought me my first Christmas tree. Known as a feather tree, it was shipped to this country from Germany.

In the early 1900s the German people became concerned about the trees that were being cut for Christmas and not replanted, so the forerunner of the artificial tree was born. The limbs with feathers were assembled in individual homes or cottages, then taken to the factory to be attached to a pine trunk, which was then wrapped in thin brown paper. My parents related that my first tree cost $3.50.

On my very first Christmas there was a doll seated in a wicker child's rocker. I later named her Margie. That same year Santa brought me a teddy bear, also manufactured in Germany, a set of building blocks and storybooks. I still have the chair, the blocks and the books. A reproduction of the doll is placed at the base of the tree.

My Christmas tree was always decorated the night before Christmas and used every year until 1941. After that my father decided we should use live trees, which were set out after the holidays.

This year my 64-year-old feather tree has been brought out of its storage box. My spouse of 41 years helped me refurbish my tree. I brought out the old decorations and decorated my tree once again. To me it's beautiful and I

LOVE IT. December 23, 1986

Designs Tree From A Green Window Shade

In our family it is not Christmas without a tree. It is a tradition we never break. It goes back to that cold, bleak winter when Grandpa and Grandma spent their first Christmas on the treeless Kansas Plains. They were homesick for the happy holiday festivities back in Germany, where they were very poor, but still had a tree with a few gifts, cookies, songs and dances. Here in Kansas there were no hills covered with evergreens.

In their two-room half-dugout, half-frame shack, Grandma had a prize possession: two green shades for the bedroom windows. Without a word to Grandma, who was busy in the kitchen baking a few old-country Christmas cookies, Grandpa slipped out into the dugout barn with one of the green shades. He found a small cottonwood sapling growing out by the creek. He made a little stand and cut Grandma's window shade into shreds and tied them carefully to the branches in evergreen fashion.

He made six makeshift candleholders from some tin cans, cutting the scraps that were left into little pieces. He strung them and field corn to hang around the tree.

Then Grandpa tied the only gifts he had for Grandma, a small sack of hard candy and a pound of coffee, to the tree. On Christmas Eve he carried the tree proudly into the house.

Grandma was delighted and never said a word about the sacrificed window shade. She added the only gifts she had for Grandpa, hand-knitted socks and a pair of mittens made from a worn-out blanket.

It was a poor tree, but it was green, and it meant Christmas to that homesick young couple. Together they sang the traditional Christmas songs and danced around the little tree.

Grandpa and Grandma have long since gone to their eternal rest. But with that tradition behind us, we always have to have a green Christmas

TREE. December 25, 1979

Children Save Money To Buy Special Present

During the Christmas season I am reminded of the wonderful Christmas holidays I shared with my parents, three sisters and two brothers while growing up in a small central Wisconsin community.

Fifteen years ago on a Friday evening in mid-December, I walked with my brothers, sisters and other shoppers past the few small shops and stores located on the three blocks of our community's Main Street. Snowflakes were falling, causing our cheeks to redden and the tips of our ears to sting.

In my pocket my hand tightly clutched the $45 we had saved to buy an artificial Christmas tree for our parents. They had wanted one for several years but had little money left during the expensive holiday season.

To get the money, we first sold some old coins my sister and I had collected. We were disappointed to receive only 40 cents beyond the face value of the coins, a total of $2, but it was a start. To raise the rest of the money we had shoveled sidewalks, sold Christmas cards, baby-sat and done other menial errands and jobs. As we looked into the hardware store we saw it—a Christmas tree more startling than any of us imagined possible. The long-needled tree, well over six feet tall, was adorned with royal blue lights and satin balls, giving it a majestic appearance. Silver and gold garlands hung from its boughs like strands of fine jewels, and a snow white angel shone from the top of the tree.

The week before Christmas my parents found the tree set up in the corner of the living room. We felt proud as our mother and father admired the tree, commenting it was the most beautiful Christmas tree they had ever seen.

When I return home each Christmas morning to celebrate the holiday with my family, I still have a special feeling for the majestic Christmas tree that dominates our living room, stirred by the memory of six children experiencing the joy of the Christmas SPIRIT. December 20, 1983

181

The Children's Tree

Several years ago, we had so much bad luck we decided to try our luck in the land where people told about money growing on trees. We sold what little we had, bought a used car and started out.

When we got to Arizona all we could find to do was pick cotton. We had a 10-year-old boy and an 8-year-old girl. At Christmas time we were 1,500 miles from home, living in a tent, discouraged and lonesome with very little money. We decided to get the children one gift and a pair of blankets for ourselves. We told the children we wouldn't have a Christmas tree and they didn't say much about it.

The afternoon we went to Phoenix to get their gifts, we gave them 15 cents each to go to the show. When we returned, the sight almost broke my heart. They had decorated a big, dead weed with balls of cotton and tinfoil. Each had bought me a pretty hankie and a cigar for their daddy. Bud had a little doll for Sis and she had a whistle for him. I just fell across the bed and cried, vowing that wherever I was on Christmas I would fix some kind of tree.

The children are married and gone now. But I will never forget those two children who believed in Christmas enough to fix up a weed for a
CHRISTMAS TREE. December 17, 1957

Her First Tree Was Like Charlie Brown's

When I was 12, there were eight of us children, and we were poor as could be. As Christmas drew near the beautiful trees came to the little store where we traded. Our grocer, Mr. Burkholder, knew everyone and most of their business as well. Every day I would stop by and dream over those trees. We'd never had one before and I wanted one so badly. I watched as they disappeared one by one, until Christmas Eve, when there was just one tree left. It was a little bitty thing. I guess no one else would have it.

I said, "Mr. Burkholder, now that it's Christmas Eve, what are you going to do with that little tree?"

I suppose he could see by the longing in my eyes that I wanted it, and that kindly man said, "I'm going to give it to you, Sissy."

Oh boy! I thanked him, grabbed up my tree, ran home as fast as I could go and flung open the door yelling, "Mama, Mama, see what I got."

When she saw that tree I suppose she saw a twin to something like a Charlie Brown tree, for all she said was, "OH!"

Our decorations were tin can lids and tin foil from gum wrappers we'd picked up, plus any little shiny thing we could scrounge, but it was so pretty. It was OUR TREE. I showed it to Dad as soon as he got home from work. To this day I don't know what he thought or how long he'd been saving the $2 he gave me, saying, "Buy something for Christmas."

It was time for the stores to close, but I ran the three blocks to town. I bought Mom, Dad and my brothers and sisters each a gift and had a few cents for hard candy. I wrapped each gift in brown sack paper and pinned or tied them to the little tree. Those little kids were tickled pink.

If I had the most gorgeous tree on Earth today, it just couldn't possibly be as pretty or mean as much as my little Charlie Brown Christmas

TREE. December 25, 1973

Christmas Trees

To these city streets, the forests are now being trucked in. They come piled up high, green as summer, their every bough asserting an affinity with sky. Once they thrusted upward to claim for festoons the angel hair of clouds, and for their stars Sirius or Polaris. Several ball-like moons have hung on them, and there were no bars between them and the snow. They will be domesticated soon with plastic deer, glass birds and cardboard angels and crepe frills of red and green. Yet sometimes, suddenly, they will exude a perfume—piercing, austere—as though a wind were blowing from the hills.

HELEN HARRINGTON. December 13, 1955

New Home—New Tree

When I was a small child we moved from our Wisconsin home to Kansas. We were delighted with our new home—until the Christmas season approached. Then we wondered how we could ever have Christmas when there wasn't one Christmas tree in the whole town.

Back in Wisconsin, my father had only to go up on the hill behind our house to find a perfect tree. And if the snow was not too deep, we children were permitted to go along and help select the tree—a very special event. Now, a Christmas without a deep green fir tree seemed a gloomy prospect, indeed.

However, our mother was one of the most resourceful women I have ever known, always equal to any emergency. She said we would have a tree—a real Kansas one. Our curiosity grew and grew, until the day before Christmas when she announced the time had come to decorate the tree. Mother brought in a branch from an old peach tree, shaped it up, set it in a block and painted it with starch. We children were given cotton batting and told to cover the tree with snowflakes. That evening we popped corn and strung cranberries (they were 10 cents a quart those days) and made stars out of tin foil—and never did we have a nicer tree than our

KANSAS ONE. December 15, 1953

A Tree For Baby

We have a Christmas tradition that is very special at our house. Whenever a new baby is due soon after the Christmas season, we put up the "baby tree."

It's a small, homemade tree, and its only decorations are the star on top and a tiny red-and-white striped stocking. We all place a small gift for the expected baby under this tree.

We will be using our tree this year for a grandchild expected shortly after the first of the year. This time, I will be able to put up the tree in my own home because the expecting parents will be in our home for Christmas.

We think our baby tree is a unique

IDEA. December 15, 1970

Way To Tell Them

I have often heard folks wish they knew how to distinguish the various evergreen trees, so from a reliable nurseryman I obtained these facts:

The white pine has five needles in a bundle, and the scales on the cones are thickened at the top.

The Scotch pine has two bluish green, short needles in a bundle. The fir has an erect cone and flat-spreading needles scattered singly. The Austrian pine has two long, dark green needles in a bunch. The Norway spruce has large hanging cones; its scattering needles point all ways. Hemlock has small hanging cones and the sprays are flat. Arbor-vitae has flat branches; cones are few-scaled with only two seeds under each. The red cedar, in spite of its name, has bluish berries and a sharp, prickly spray. The pitch pine has dark stiff needles arranged in threes.

TREE LOVER. December 20, 1941

The Place To Be

After much eager anticipation we finally got our Christmas tree put up and decorated. Our 6-year-old sighed in admiration, "I just wish I was a present so I could sit under the Christmas

TREE!" December 20, 1966

Have Two Trees

The toddler at our house couldn't understand why he couldn't help trim the big, beautiful Christmas tree when the older children were allowed to handle the shining globes and little angels and gleaming star. So there were tears and tantrums in a time of joy.

But Daddy solved the problem in less than five minutes. He fastened some of the branches that had been removed from the big tree onto a board and presto! The littlest one had a tree all his own on which to hang tinsel, foil and plastic pretties in lop-sided array.

Don't have tears and a messy tree—have

TWO TREES! December 21, 1954

Try This On Your Tree

A saturated solution of Epsom salts dropped on the branches of the Christmas tree will dry and look like frost. It may also be used on glass of any kind, on electric light bulbs, etc. It makes a pretty, inexpensive decoration for a small tree. Other homemade decorations are nut shells, sticks, spools, etc., covered with tin foil or bright paper. Cutout pictures, paper chains, strings of popcorn, little cut-out stars, bells, trees and stockings. The children will enjoy making them and will think less of what they are going to receive for Christmas and where it is hidden. Keep them busy and they will be happy and out of mischief.

MRS. R. December 20, 1930

Tree Has Steps

I remember many Christmases when Santa had to make do, but we had a mother who didn't tell us we were poor. We were happy, even though we didn't have things like other people.

The time I remember most was when we had a Christmas tree made from a stepladder. The legs and steps were covered with red and green crepe paper. A barrel hoop was nailed on top, with a red bell hanging in the center. Tinsel was woven around the legs. It was beautiful.

One year in my own home I decorated a stepladder and strung lights on it. While there were a lot of comments and compliments, it didn't measure up to the one in my

CHILDHOOD. December 17-25, 1973

Christmas Favors

Besides the usual large family Christmas tree, I put up a small tree for children. I adorn it with candy canes, cookies, chewing gum, popcorn balls and small toys. Beneath the tree I place a small pair of scissors so each small guest can snip off the favor they

DECIDE ON. December 17, 1957

Wrap It Up

Chapter 14

W HAT WOULD CHRISTMAS be without lots of festive wrapping paper? In days gone by—when paper was hard to find—presents were often placed in stockings unwrapped. Today, however, no present seems complete without a cheery print and a festive bow. Over the years, readers have shared lots of wrapping hints with me, including how to secure packages for mailing and tips on making your own paper.

Funny, though, no one yet has suggested how to keep the babies from paying more attention to the wrappings than the presents on Christmas Day!

Christmas Wrappings
I tied the package beautifully
With tinseled stars galore—

A bow of red, a spray of pine,
How could one ask for more—

I gazed with rapture at my work
Yes, I was filled with pride—

Until I found that I had left
The Christmas gift outside!

Ora Kehn, December 23, 1944

Gift Wrapping With Personality
For an unusual, yet inexpensive gift wrap, use bright-colored tissue paper. On it, carefully glue a variety of snowflake designs cut from an assortment of lacy-white paper that you may have on hand.

A Christmas tree, or any other holiday pattern, may be arranged from the cut-outs. Sequins, colored stars or glitter may be used for additional beauty—giving the packaged gift a personality all its

OWN. December 2, 1969

Up In The Air
With the cost of gifts soaring so these days, and with many on a limited income, the answer is often money for the youngsters. Here's a novel way to "wrap" it.

Put your bill in a balloon, then blow it up and tie the end. Using a pretty ribbon with a name tag attached, tie the balloon to the Christmas

TREE. December 1, 1970

Giant Gift Wrap

I use trash bags for big, hard-to-wrap packages such as a tricycle. They can be decorated with big, red nylon net ribbons and colorful seals. After the gift is opened, the trash bag can be "recycled" by using it to hold discarded gift wrap and ribbon. It sure makes cleanup easier for

MRS. SANTA. December 26, 1972

Christmas Package Tips

Names and addresses on packages will always be legible if you write plainly in ink, let dry thoroughly and then cover with a coating of clear nail polish.

To mail homemade fudge successfully, pour while warm into a tin that has been lined with several thicknesses of waxed paper. Leave enough paper to cover the top. The fudge can be lifted out in one piece and will stay fresh longer.

To pack cookies, cut the top of a milk carton on three sides. When filled, seal tight.

Cake or cookies will stay fresh longer if packed in marshmallows. They act as humidors.

MRS. SANTA. December 6, 1952

That "Christmasy" Look

A novel way of wrapping Christmas packages is to buy the tiny gilt sleigh bells that are sold by the dozen and tie them to the ends of the ribbon or cord. Tiny sprays of evergreen tucked in the wrappings of Christmas packages add a delightful finishing touch. Large chocolate drops wrapped in tinfoil and tucked in the corners of a Christmas package will delight the heart of any child. To give a Christmas touch to a large package, write "Merry Christmas" on it with glue and sprinkle artificial snow or clipped green tissue paper over the glue words.

LOIS CANNON. December 19, 1931

Gift-Wrap Ideas

Here are some ideas for wrapping Christmas packages:

Wrap large, flat packages in dark, solid-colored tissue paper. Cut a circle from plain white construction paper, using a salad plate as a guide. Glue the circle to the center of the package. Now cut out two black eyes, a black stovepipe hat, nose, smiling lips and a crooked pipe. Assemble these on the circle to make a jaunty snowman and glue them on securely.

For gifts of lingerie, scarves, hankies or other small cloth items, save cardboard rolls from paper towels, waxed paper and so forth. Slip the gift into the roll, wrap in white tissue. Fasten a red ribbon to one end, then wind it around the roll in candy-stick fashion and fasten at the other end.

Wrap small, flat boxes in plain white paper, and glue a green Christmas tree cut from construction paper to the top. Cut bits of bright paper and foil, and glue them in scattered array to the tree as ornaments.

It really doesn't take more time to wrap these gifts than to tie the usual fancy bows—but your friends will think you took extra time to make their gifts look

SPECIAL. December 14, 1954

Children Create Wrapping Paper

Celebrating holidays and traditions are important to our family, but sometimes it's difficult to find ways for preschoolers to participate.

Here's one suggestion: Make wrapping paper. One year we used the paper itself as gifts. Other years all our gifts were wrapped in homemade paper.

Start with white tissue paper and food coloring in plastic squeeze bottles. Stack four or five sheets of tissue paper opened flat. Lay it on top of a table covered thickly with newspapers to absorb extra liquid. Even very young children can simply squeeze blobs of color onto the tissue. The colors absorb and spread quickly. That's all there is to it.

Older children will enjoy putting color onto a piece of sponge and blotting it on the paper. Add a little water to the paper and colors will blend and spread in new ways. Potato prints can also be done in this way.

Results are really colorful and pretty. Because several sheets are done at one time, a lot of paper can be decorated quickly. You're only limited by the space you have to let the paper dry. The children are thrilled when packages begin to appear under the tree wrapped in their

CREATIONS. December 8, 1981

Original Wrappings

Since my husband is in the Air Force, our parents aren't able to see our children often or know much about their schoolwork. So I save their arithmetic papers, spelling tests, pictures they draw, and use them to wrap or to pack Christmas gifts. Sometimes I think the grandmas find the packing as interesting as the

GIFTS. December 5, 1961

I Like To Wrap Gifts

I'll have fun wrapping my presents this year. I have the gayest wrapping paper and the prettiest seals. And if I'm not mistaken there's a box of leftovers that can be used. I guess most folks get a kick out of wrapping presents—goodness knows I do. I like to make a package look so beautiful outside that the fellow who gets it won't want to open it for awhile. I do like those fancy fixings.

MARY. December 18, 1937

Smart Wrapping Santa

When you wrap those Christmas gifts, add a bunch of bitter-sweet in the ribbon bow, or perhaps a sprig of holly if you live where it is available. Evergreen and cedar also add a woody, decorative touch. If the gift is for children, it will be twice as welcome if you loop an all-day sucker or a stick of candy in the bow.

MRS. A.H. December 6, 1941

Ideas For "Wrappings"

A sprig of holly, evergreen, or cluster of pine cones placed in the top of your Christmas box adds much to the atmosphere of a gift package. Gifts from the kitchen may be cleverly packed in numerous ways. Enameled and decorated tin boxes, coffee cans—even cold cream jars may be used. Cottage cheese and ice cream cartons may be decorated and used. These are especially handy for puddings and candies. Waxed paper is invaluable to preserve the moisture of cakes and candies.

MRS. L.H. December 15, 1934

Holly Humor

Chapter 15

*K*IDS SAY THE funniest things... especially at Christmas time. The excitement created by Santa's impending arrival has also led to peculiar antics by more than one youngster. I couldn't resist including a chapter of these funny little stories that are sure to bring out the Christmas spirit in even the biggest Scrooge.

If you've had your fill of the Christmas rush, settle down with a nice cold glass of eggnog and have a chuckle courtesy of these classic examples of holiday humor.

Sounds Cheap

Only a short time after Christmas catalogs arrived, my small son brought me a list that filled two large sheets of paper.

He told me, "Mommy, I have my list all fixed, and it only comes to 89 cents and about

40 DOLLARS." December 4, 1973

Shari's Mistletoe

The Christmas decorating was nearly complete; shiny ornaments, candles and greenery lent holiday spirit throughout the house. As Mother fastened a sprig of mistletoe in the doorway, she explained to little Shari and Staci that anyone standing under the mistletoe would receive a kiss.

The girls anxiously waited for Daddy to come home from work and raced to greet him. "Hurry, Daddy," Shari said. "Let's go stand under the

TIPPY-TOE!" December 7, 1971

No Chimney

When we moved into our new house last year, it was the first time my tiny daughter had lived in a house without a fireplace.

On Christmas Eve, we were surprised when she put on her coat and headed for the front door. When we asked her what she was doing, she said, "I'm going to Grandma's. I'm not spending Christmas Eve in a house that doesn't have a chimney to let Santa Claus

IN." December 1, 1970

Is Santa Related?

Our little great-grandson came home from first grade with this question, "Mama, if Jesus is our Brother and God our Father, is Santa Claus our

GRANDPA?" December 23, 1950

Playin' Reindeer

One of our boys has always had a lively imagination and lots of energy. Every day brought something different! But I was puzzled when I found him well-smeared with a cold remedy salve—the kind we call "Vicks" for short. "Just what are you doing?" I demanded.

"I'm playing reindeer," was the matter-of-fact reply.

More puzzled than ever, I asked, "What's that got to do with wasting half a bottle of Vicks?"

"Mama, you should know," replied the little fellow cheerfully. "I'm
VIXEN!" December 1, 1970

Baby Jesus Had No Bottle

The class was preparing to present "The Friendly Beasts," where each animal is present in the manger with the Baby Jesus. We were almost ready for curtain time when my little red-haired "Joseph" looked at me with big, blue eyes and inquired, "Where is the bottle for Baby Jesus?"

Thinking carefully, I replied that I didn't know if bottles were invented at that time.

He persisted, "What did His mother do, hold Him up under the
COW?" December 8, 1987

Had Politics In Mind

Just before Christmas 1980, our granddaughter, age 9, was in the local supermarket. Santa was there asking all the children what they wanted and passing out an assortment of chocolate animals.

When our granddaughter opened her sack, there was a chocolate elephant. Having watched political campaigning on TV, she gave Santa a straight look and said in a loud voice, "Oh, Santa, I didn't know you were a
REPUBLICAN!" December 8, 1981

Noel Becomes Leon

A small town near us put up their Christmas decorations, including beautiful garlands hung above Main Street with NOEL in large letters. These garlands faced toward midtown, but were backward to approaching traffic.

My neighbor and her small son, Leon, who had just learned to print his name, were nearing the town when he started yelling, "Look, Mommy! They knew I was coming and hung me over the
STREET." December 25, 1979

Where Was He Born?

When the 4-year-olds' Sunday School teacher became ill, I was asked to teach the class.

I asked the children if they knew a Bible story. Callie said, "I know the one about Jesus being born in a
STAPLE." December 8, 1992

Didn't Fool Him

We always take advantage of the Christmas season to discipline our son, aged 3. To make the idea that Santa was watching him more realistic we purchased a dime-store mask. We took turns wearing it and looking in the window at various times during the evenings. We were delighted with the better behavior that resulted.

One day my husband and I were having an argument, when our son looked up and said, "Now it's my turn to wear the
SANTA FACE." December 9, 1950

Direct Approach

Before Christmas 3-year-old Neil was told by his mother to pick up his toys or Santa wouldn't bring him the train he wanted. After a moment's hesitation, Neil replied, "I'm getting tired of this Santa business. Why don't we just go downtown and buy a
TRAIN?" December 4-11, 1962

Searches For Heaven

A few years ago, I owned and operated a small bakery. Of course, my son Rusty knew everyone had to have cake on his or her birthday.

A week before Christmas (the weather was chilly and windy), we discovered that 3-year-old Rusty was missing. After calling all the local stores to no avail, we called the police. After a couple of hours had passed with no one seeing him, he walked in with a disappointed look on his face. Still angry and worried about him, I said, probably too loudly, "Where in the world have you been?"

He looked at me with those innocent eyes and said, "Well, Mom, I was just looking for heaven, so we'd know where to take Jesus' birthday

CAKE." December 18, 1984

Famous Trio

The teacher of the first-grade Sunday School class brought in the nativity scene figures, individually wrapped, so the children could have the fun of opening and identifying each figure.

When little Jimmy's turn came, he was stuck. "One of the three what?" his teacher prompted.

Jimmy thought a moment, then answered brightly,

"MUSKETEERS!" December 12, 1961

Don't Let Mama Hear!

Eavesdropping can be fun! My 6-year-old nephew and his 9-year-old cousin were on the other side of the house discussing Christmas and Santa Claus.

"You know there really isn't a Santa Claus, don't you, Jimmy?" said the 9-year-old.

"Yes," said my nephew. "I've know for a long time, but I haven't told Mama yet. She still believes there is one."

EAVESDROPPER. December 18, 1948

Parents Aren't Rich

My daughter and her husband have two sweet little girls. Brenda is 11 and Teresa is 9 years old. Brenda has accepted the fact that there is no Santa Claus, but Teresa will not believe it.

One day Teresa came running home from school, saying to her mother, "Mama, the girls in my class say there isn't any Santa Claus, it is just your mother and father. I said, 'No way! My folks just couldn't afford all those toys I got on Christmas!'"

Such is the faith of precious little

GRANDCHILDREN. December 23, 1980

Mischievous Child Opens The Gifts

The Christmas that stands out in my memory was a near disaster. We were entertaining some friends at a Christmas Eve party. I gave 4-year-old Jimmy a bath and put him to bed about 7:30, an hour before the guests were due.

Knowing Jimmy's penchant for getting into mischief, I decided to check on him. I found his bed empty, and he was nowhere in sight.

We had a big Christmas tree in a corner of the family room, and I felt sure that was where he would be. Sure enough, he was sitting on the floor under the tree, amid the bright packages and boxes. He had partially opened one he knew was his. I wanted to get back to my guests, so I told him to go ahead and open the package, then go to bed. After some time had passed, I asked my husband to check on Jimmy. He was back in a few minutes— white as a sheet! He motioned for me to follow him. He pointed to a small shape lying in an ocean of papers, ribbon, strings and name cards. Jimmy had opened everything in sight. Worn out, he had gone to sleep hugging a big stuffed bear. He looked so innocent we couldn't be angry.

Needless to say, we spent Christmas morning trying to sort out the mess and discover who had sent what to

WHOM. December 18, 1984

198

Waits For Mistletoe Kiss

When our 5-year-old nephew was at our house, he stood for a few minutes under the mistletoe hanging above the door.

Then he came over and asked, "If you stand under mistletoe, aren't you supposed to get a kiss?"

"Yes," we said.

He said, "I stood under it and I didn't feel
ANYTHING." December 17, 1985

Snow Comes First

My sister's great-granddaughter, 5-year-old Amy, was caught in the yard throwing handfuls of Tide in the air. She was spanked and sent into the house.

Tearfully, Amy said, "I was just making snow so Santa Claus would come
SOONER." November 24, 1981

Addition To Scene

A Christmas tradition at our household is to set up a small nativity set. Through the Christmas season, our children were always allowed to handle the figurines as we read or told the story. Our children commented on how real it made Christmas.

Recently a new object was added to the scene. Our 3-year-old grandson placed his little four-wheel drive pickup in the scene. I heard him say, "You can ride in my four-wheeler, Mary. Den you won't be so tired."

Wouldn't Mary have been
SURPRISED. December 20, 1988

Mixed Holidays

The first time 2 1/2-year-old Nancy saw Santa Claus, she cried gleefully "Treats or
TRICKS!" December 20, 1960

It's Time For Mistletoe

One of my efforts to get people to "reach out and touch someone," especially at Christmas time, is to hang mistletoe over the doorway. Now I believe this is one tradition that will be carried on by the next generation.

Tonight, my 6-year-old grandson, David, asked, "Grandma, when are you going to put the kissing bush
UP?" December 20, 1988

One Deer Missing!

These modern children! Last Christmas I was reading "The Night Before Christmas" to my small nephews. When I finished the part, "Now, Dasher! now, Dancer! now, Prancer and Vixen! On, Comet! on, Cupid! on, Donner and Blitzen," Billy excitedly exclaimed, "Why, where's
RUDOLPH!" December 20, 1952

Carol Sing

We are laughing at our niece's version of two Christmas carols. She was singing, and when asked what she would like to sing, the 3-year-old answered, "Let's sing 'O Holy Nightmare.'"

Later her older sister had to inform her that another song was "Away in a Manger," not the "Lone
RANGER." December 12, 1961

Limited Appreciation

My mother used to tell me about the little girl who received a comb and brush set for Christmas from her aunt.

"You must write a note and thank Auntie," her mother said.

After considerable thought, the little girl wrote: "Dear Auntie Rose, Thank you for the comb and brush set. I've always wanted one, but not
VERY MUCH." December 22, 1951

Santa Seemed Just Like "Family" To Her

My late husband played the role of Santa Claus for many years. He went to church, club meetings and also private homes by request.

One year—when our youngest daughter, Linda, was almost 5 years old and her friend, Luanne, was a few months younger—we were at church on Christmas Eve. The Christmas program was over, and Santa appeared in his red suit, handing out bags of candy and nuts. Luanne became very much afraid when Santa got closer. Our daughter Linda, who still believed in Santa Claus, said: "Don't be afraid, Luanne, he's got Daddy's shoes
ON!" December 21, 1993

Christmas Song

My 4-year-old granddaughter asked me if I wanted to hear the Christmas song she learned. "Yes," I answered, and she began to sing, "We three kings of glory and
TAR." December 13, 1960

Who's That?

Late in life, I married a bachelor whose name was Christmas. My name is Mary, and people think I'm joking when I tell them I am Mary
CHRISTMAS. December 15, 1970

Changed His Name

After the first-graders exchanged names for our gift exchange, one little boy told his mother, "Mother, my name isn't Andrew any more." Somewhat surprised, his mother asked, "What is your name?"

"I don't know," he answered. "It's on this paper. Teacher said we were going to
CHANGE NAMES!" December 2, 1958

Needs The Money

Six-year-old Danny was visiting his uncle when he discovered a loose tooth. Uncle Ben tied a string to the tooth and painlessly pulled it out. That night a bright silver dollar was planted under Danny's pillow.

"The Good Fairy put it there," Uncle Ben explained later. Danny asked whether money would be left if he lost other teeth. We assured him the fairies were good to good little folks.

That afternoon I noticed Danny standing before a mirror with a thread tied around a front tooth.

"I've decide to pull another tooth now," he told me seriously. "I'm going to need at least two dollars for Christmas
SHOPPING." December 6-13, 1966

Santa Claus Forgets

Twenty-three years ago when our son was only 4, we attended a community Christmas program at a rural school. There was a huge decorated tree loaded with gifts and sacks of treats for everyone.

A special Santa, who knew each child by name, was on hand to ask each one what he or she wanted for Christmas. When Santa asked our son the big question, Jack replied, "You ought to know, I told you Saturday at
SEARS." December 9, 1980

Kissing Weed

Our 3-year-old watched with glee the numerous scuffles under the mistletoe at the holiday gathering. Later as we sat visiting, Mister Three climbed into my lap, got a firm grip around my neck, and groped in his pocket. His eyes told me there was mischief afoot, but I was hardly prepared for a handful of mistletoe berries being firmly squashed on top of my head. After a struggle he succeeded in favoring me with several juicy kisses, after which he triumphantly chirped, "Ha, ha, I kissed you under the
MISTLE WEED." December 23, 1958

Wears Wig To Christmas Dance

Boy, do I remember a dance! This was a Christmas dance in junior high. I was in the eighth grade, and my sister was in the seventh. Mom got us pretty dresses of velvet, and I felt rich.

My younger sister, Brenda, wanted more. She wanted to wear Mom's curly haired wig. Patiently Mom put the wig on her. Oh, did Brenda look pretty! She was a little stiff, I guess, because she was afraid the wig would fall off.

As I remember, Sis got through the first few dances pretty well. Then, wouldn't you know it, they played "Wipe Out." Well, let's just say her hair took up the dance. Before I knew it, I saw Brenda's wig flying across the dance floor. She grabbed the wig and ran to the girls' bathroom. I found her there, tears running down her face, trying to put the wig back on her head.

We departed the dance early. At 12, my sister found out your own hair is much better for
DANCING. December 4, 1990

"It'll Be Hard To Tell Daddy"

It's near Christmas again, and at our house it's beginning to seem a lot like Christmas already.

My husband is always first to see Santa Claus downtown. He always buys a tree too tall for the house. He enjoys buying and wrapping presents, and sees Santa peeking in the window. He's the first to hear sleigh bells on Christmas Eve, leaving the children round-eyed in wonder. He's always awake first on Christmas morning, waiting for the kids to wake up so he can spring from his bed to join them in a race to the tree. He's really a big kid at heart.

This year the girls have already started asking that age-old question, "Who is Santa Claus, Mommy?" I decided to level with them and tell them what they had long suspected. I told them how they could be in on the big secret and we wouldn't tell baby sister.

My eight-year-old looked at me gravely and said, "I'll sure hate it when you have to tell Daddy about
SANTA CLAUS." December 1, 1970

203

"Why Not, Mama?"

Just before Christmas a young mother was telling her 3-year-old daughter about Santa and his reindeer. She was suddenly stopped by the little girls' question, "Well, why don't they call them snowdeer,

MAMA?" December 17-24, 1968

Merry Mary

When writing my Christmas letters and cards I sign, "Merry Christmas." My preschool daughter, Mary (having an older sister, Susie) brightly asked, "Mommy, why do you always write 'Mary Christmas'? Why not 'Susie

CHRISTMAS'?" December 4-11, 1973

Christmas Geography

We took our little niece, 4, to a football game. When the announcer said that the team would defend the north goal, Janie leapt to her feet and shouted, "That's where

SANTA CLAUS LIVES!" December 13, 1952

Holiday Hints

Chapter 16

*H*OW CAN YOU take your Christmas tree out without dropping needles everywhere? Which Christmas plants are poisonous? How do you keep your Christmas lights from getting all tangled up? These readers' hints make holiday chores easier. They also provide useful information for keeping kids and pets safe during what can be a potentially dangerous time of year.

Read the helpful hints on the following pages before the season gets into full swing. I guarantee you'll find time-saving tips that will give you more time for carolling and kinship (or maybe even a little mistletoe testing)!

Christmas Tree Use

Your ex-Christmas tree branches will be fine protection for your outdoor plants, as they are light and will permit circulation of air. Mulching is not to keep the plants warm, but to maintain an even soil temperature. It is not needed until the soil is frozen hard.

BEE. January 1, 1949

Fun Without A Tree

If there will be no Christmas tree, it is fun to put each person's gifts in a group by themselves. Blindfold them in turn and make them unwrap their gifts, tell what each is and what it is used for. Of course, someone must be handy to see that nothing is broken and that the card is replaced on the gift so there will be no mistake in the thank-you letters.

It truly is lots of fun to hear some of the guesses.

COLORADO. December 20, 1930

Opens With Ease

When you seal a box or Christmas package with tape, place a length of cord under the tape, allowing an inch or two to protrude from the end. This will make it much easier for the recipient to open the package.

Pull the cord and the tape will rip neatly down the

MIDDLE. December 1, 1970

Wrapper Put To Use

When making pie crust or roll-out cookies, cut the end off a large size bread wrapper. Split it open, dampen countertop and place wrapper (printed side down) on it. Smooth out air bubbles. When finished, just roll up and throw away. If there are no holes in wrapper, shake off crumbs and place in freezer until next

TIME. December 12, 1978

Water Fireproofs The Christmas Tree

No chemical has proved as effective for fireproofing a Christmas tree as plain water, which keeps the tree naturally moist and thus resistant to flame. The best answer is to buy a fresh tree and then keep it fresh by standing it in water.

If the tree is fresh, the needles will feel moist as you run your hand over the bough. If needles fall when you move or shake the tree, it is already dry and no longer able to absorb water.

As soon as you bring the tree home, throw cold water all over it. Then cut off the trunk about one inch slantwise, to open pores for drawing up water. Set the tree in water and keep it cool until it comes indoors for trimming. The first day a five- to six-foot tree is placed in water, it may take up more than a quart of water. Replenish water daily because the tree may take up a cup of water every day in a warm

ROOM. December 17-24, 1963

Self-Service Drinks

Our holiday means a short weekend with a dozen house guests. A real convenience for me is my big coffee percolator. I fill it with water, plug it in and set out instant coffee, tea bags, instant hot chocolate mix and cups. Last year I added a jar of instant fruit-flavored drink that can be served hot or cold. Our guests can drink what they prefer without feeling they are a

BOTHER. December 13, 1977

Fingers Stay Clean

When making cookies, use a paper towel for the initial greasing, then clean the cookie sheets before adding a new batch. Crumbs remove easily with the greasy paper towel; you re-grease the pans at the same time and save your hands. Make a final cleanup easy by using the towel to clean the sheets of crumbs before washing. Then just throw the towel

AWAY! December 13, 1977

Bright Strings

While you are untangling the strings of Christmas lights this year, plan to make it easy on yourself next year. After Christmas, roll the strings of lights around empty cardboard tubes your gift wrapping came on this year. This makes for neater storage,

TOO. December 2, 1975

Carry Tree Out

It's easy to carry out your tree after the holiday if you cut off all the branches with your pruning clippers and put them in a carton to be carried out separately. The skeleton of your tree won't scratch walls or

DOORS. December 27, 1960

Timmy Buckles Up Now

I thought someone might be helped by this idea at Christmas time. My little grandson, Timmy, never wanted to be buckled into his car seat. He would fight it every time.

Last Christmas a neighbor gave him a little truck. The neighbor tied a little toy man into the driver's seat—just for fun. Timmy was so excited about it, he said, "Look, he's got his seat belt on."

After that, Timmy buckled up with no fuss and even began to tell others to use their seat belts. Perhaps someone could use this idea—it might save a

LIFE. December 6, 1983

Recycle Old Flowers

Recycle your old and faded artificial flowers into attractive Christmas wreaths or bouquets. First, wash them with soap and water. Dry and spray paint them with colors of your choice. Red blossoms and leaves touched with silver or gold accents make an attractive

ARRANGEMENT. December 2-9, 1975

Save The Table Top

With a coping saw, cut a set of three hot dish protectors from plasterboard. Transfer designs of butterflies, birds or any other design, color with crayons, then shellac over them. These make a pretty gift.

MRS. WILL UMPHRES. December 15, 1934

For Next Christmas

Write the name and full address on the back of each Christmas card as you put your Christmas things away. Then tie your cards together and you'll have no trouble next year hunting addresses and trying to remember

ALL YOUR FRIENDS. January 5, 1952

A Christmas Picnic

A group of children will have a peck of fun during the holidays if you give them a Christmas picnic. Pack sandwiches, cookies, paper napkins and forks and spoons in shoe boxes wrapped with Christmas paper and tied with pretty ribbons. Give each child one of these picnic boxes and a place to have their picnic. The warm basement is a good place and may be decorated to suit the occasion. Use the lids of the boxes for trays to eat on.

CHRISTMAS LADY. December 13, 1941

Spools Decorate Tree

If you have a lot of empty thread spools, here's a way to put them to use. I cut strips from my bright-colored prints and wrap them around the spool. I overlap them a little and put a dab of glue on them to hold them in place. Then I put bright-colored yarn through the spool and tie them on my Christmas tree. I get many compliments on them. Let the children help; it's

FUN. November 11, 1975

Needle-Catcher

When you put up your Christmas tree spread out an old sheet and set your tree in the middle. Fold the sheet up around the tree stand and put the tree skirt over. When you take your tree down, simply unfold the sheet and it will catch all the
NEEDLES. December 3-10, 1974

Plants Can Poison Pets

Poinsettia, mistletoe, Star of Bethlehem and Christmas roses are all beautiful. But they are also toxic and should be placed where pets can look but not
TOUCH. December 6, 1983

Pretty Gift Bookmark

Any young stamp collectors on your gift list? A piece of light cardboard covered with stamps from foreign countries or commemorative United States stamps makes an appropriate bookmark. Apply several light coats of varnish over the stamps for durability. This makes an unusual stocking
STUFFER. November 11, 1975

For Christmas Cards

It's your tongue that takes the licking when you have a stack of Christmas cards to stamp and seal. Try using ice cubes instead. As the cubes melt you have a wet surface ready for moistening stamps or
FLAPS. December 8, 1951

String Styro Pebbles

If you can find some of those Styrofoam packing pebbles, or the small pieces that look like peanuts, string them and decorate the tree. They look like strings of
POPCORN. December 13, 1977

Removes Sticky Tape
If you stick decorations on your windows for the holidays, use fingernail polish remover to take off the transparent gummed tape that remains on the window after you take the decoration
DOWN. December 21-28, 1976

Fence Out Tot
To keep a toddler from pulling the glittering ornaments from the Christmas tree or upsetting the tree, put the tree in baby's playpen—and keep the baby outside,
OF COURSE! December 22, 1953

"Bake" The Cotton
When making cushions for Christmas, if you lack feathers for filling, try cotton batting. Cut into small squares and heat in a baking pan in the oven; it will almost double in bulk and makes a fluffy filling.
MRS. N.D. December 12, 1931

For Holiday Stains
Do you know what to do if some of that Christmas punch should spill on your pretty rayon dresses? Act fast—these stains are almost colorless at first—but they turn brown and are almost impossible to remove if they are allowed to stand, or if they're heated with ironing. For washable rayon, launder with warm water to dilute and remove the stain rapidly.
MRS. A.K. December 24, 1949

Pocket Surprises
Add fun to a gift of clothing for a child by stuffing pockets with candy, gum or small
TOYS. December 17-24, 1963

Christmas Cans

I have been saving my potato chip cans and have been using them for hiding the shape of Christmas presents. I put the small packages inside the cylinder along with paper to prevent rattling. I paint the cans red, green, blue or gold. Then I take the white corrugated paper from the inside and cut it curved on one end and straight on the other end to look like snow drifts. I glue this on the upper part of the can. Next, I put a small hole in the top plastic disk and insert an inexpensive decoration such as a snowman or Santa Claus on a pick. I have a gift box that's decorative, fun to give and keeps them guessing till

CHRISTMAS. December 17-24, 1974

Fastens Ornaments

Use the wire tie-ons from bread wrappers to attach ornaments and lights to your Christmas tree. They will keep balls from dropping and breaking and make it easier for you to place the

LIGHTS. December 18-25, 1973

Keep 'Em Fresh

When decorating with green boughs, mistletoe or holly, keep each piece fresh days longer by sticking the stem ends into a large potato. (You can easily hide the potato among the boughs.) The moisture in the potato helps keep your decorations

GREEN. December 1, 1970

Poinsettia Care

Here's how to take care of your Christmas poinsettia: As soon as the red leaves begin to drop, place the plant in a cool temperature—around 40 to 60 degrees—and let the soil dry out for about four months.

Around May 1 the stalks should be cut back to eight inches. Take the plant out of the pot and remove all the old soil, and put it in a fresh pot just large enough to hold the roots without crowding. For soil use a mixture of one part leaf mold, one part manure, to three parts of good garden loam. After placing in new soil put the plant in a warm, light place with water enough to keep the soil moist. Start increasing the water as the foliage grows.

Late in the spring set the pot in the ground where it can get good sunlight. Next fall bring the plant indoors to a light, airy place around 60 degrees. By December your poinsettia should be lovely again and ready to brighten

CHRISTMAS '49. January 1, 1949

Easy Way To Transfer

Now is the time of year when all are busy with Christmas sewing. I have found this to be an easy way to trace patterns. Place the pattern on carbon paper with the carbon side up. Tracing over this puts the carbon marks on the back of the pattern. Now press with a hot iron and the pattern is transferred without any slipping of paper or material.

E.L.M. December 11, 1937

Make A "Home" For Toys

With Christmas near, why not prepare for the new collection of children's toys? Solve the problem of scattered toys by painting a box and pasting pictures of toys on the sides. The children will soon learn to regard the pretty box as "toy home" and realize that their toys must be kept in the box.

MIRIAM. December 13, 1941

Prevent Burned Hands

To form popcorn balls quickly—before syrup hardens—wear clean rubber gloves. Coat gloves with cooking oil. You won't burn your hands and this way it isn't so

MESSY. December 27, 1977

213

Wishbones, Pine Cones

Begin now to save the "wishbones" from fowls. Dry them well, then dip them in enamel of bright colors or in gold paint. When wrapping Christmas packages, tie them in the bow of Christmas ribbons. Pine cones may also be tinted in colors and touched with gold and used in the same way. These help make packages attractive.

MRS. B.M.R. December 13, 1941

"How Many Days Until Christmas?"

This time of year, most youngsters are asking the same question: "How many more days till Christmas?"

Several years ago my granddaughter solved the problem for her small son. She took a long strip of paper, put as many numbers as the days until Christmas, with number one being Christmas Eve. Each day the bottom number was taken off as the child did his own counting of the days.

I made one for the children next door. I cut pictures from last year's Christmas cards—Santas, trees, candles—and mounted them on a length of ribbon and numbered them. Number 1 is a Santa Claus to be taken off Christmas Eve. The counter ribbon seems to fascinate the

SMALL FRY. December 13, 1960

Moist Fruit Cake

When packing fruit cake for shipping a long distance, place a large, juicy apple with it. This keeps the cake from drying out and also improves the flavor and odor of the cake.

X.Y.Z. December 19, 1931

Thank-You Notes

Christmas brings thoughts of gifts, and after the gifts, the words of appreciation that should go promptly to the sender.

Not too many years ago, getting our children to write their

thank-you notes was a problem, until we tried a new device for motivating the note writing. Now every year each child finds, among other things in his stocking, a package of thank-you notes. Each package is different; usually the girls receive the flowery kind and the boys get those with animals or a slightly comic approach.

When the events of Christmas Day begin to slow down and a quiet time arrives, without any suggestion from us, the children can be found writing their thank-you notes on their notepaper. I don't know how this would work for other families, but at our house, it has really solved the
PROBLEM. December 20, 1960

Ribbon Dispenser

Stack spools of ribbon in an oatmeal box. Cut a slit in the box for each spool of ribbon. Tape ribbon ends to the outside when not using. You have a dispenser and all the ribbons in one
PLACE. December 3-10, 1974

Removes Tree Pitch

If you get pitch on your hands from your Christmas tree or evergreen boughs, just moisten a cotton ball with nail polish remover and rub over hands. The pitch will disappear quickly and
SAFELY. December 1-8, 1964

No Tired Christmas Tree

To keep your Christmas tree from shedding its needles, set the stem in a can of sweetened water. It will stay fresh and green for weeks. I have done this for years and my tree is as fresh when I take it down as when I set it up,
EVERGREEN. December 15, 1951

215

The True Christmas Spirit

Chapter 17

BEHIND ALL THE tinsel and trimmings, the parties and presents, lies the true spirit of Christmas. The season has become more commercialized, the gifts have gotten bigger and better, but just under the surface the knowledge that Christmas is a time to celebrate the birth of Christ and be kind to our fellow man always remains.

Fortunately, there are many things to remind us of the real reason for the holiday. A lone candle illuminating a friendly face, a child's look of wonder when he hears the story of Jesus' birth for the first time—these things will always remind us of the real meaning of Christmas.

Candle in Doorway Brings Perspective

My first Christmas away from home! How I dreaded it. And how sorry I felt for myself. It was my first year in nurses training, and the happy hustle of Christmas shopping, friends dropping in, the wonderful spicy kitchen scents of cookies and plum puddings, the secret wrapping of gifts—and so much more—were all sadly missing. And to top it off, I had to work our routine 12-hour shift. Others around were packing to go home, but not me. To make matters worse, (as if they could possibly be any worse!) we had to rise extra early to carol throughout the hospital and the home for the aged connected to it.

Self-pity is not a constructive emotion. And although I was reared in a Christian home, where the true meaning of the day was emphasized, I'm afraid my main feeling was one of resentment and pity that this was how I was to spend the day.

We were caroling in the dark corridors of the home for the aged. Slowly we passed door after closed door. Suddenly, in an open doorway stood a frail old woman. How early she must have gotten up to welcome us. The lighted candle, her only Christmas decoration, was in her hands. Its light shone on her face, reflecting all the joy of Christmas. Alone in the world, one room for her home, a life of living behind her, and yet the joy of the Christ Child's birthday was hers. How small and petty were my own feelings! How quickly my own world returned to proper perspective; how wonderful this day really was!

Many Christmases have passed since then, but never has a Christmas come that her image isn't present in my mind and heart. Each year I thank that unknown woman who, with a gentle smile and solitary candle, lit the true meaning of the day for me to last through all the

YEARS. December 17-24, 1963

Gifts That Endure

Christmas is just around the corner and will almost seem to jump at you before you know it. Are you planning to make it an

218

unforgettable one for the children? What's that? You can't afford it? Say, here's a list of gifts that each child should have every Christmas, and they cost almost nothing but a little time and effort.

First, give them the Christmas spirit. Tell them over and over the story of the Christ child. Teach them Christmas songs and verses. Give them the joy of giving. Help them plan and make simple little gifts for children less fortunate than themselves and for old people. Just the knowledge that somebody thinks of them with kindness means so much to the underprivileged. A nicely arranged box or basket containing home-made candy, popcorn balls, crackerjacks, small spice cakes, gingerbread, jelly, some fruit or anything you wish may mean a Merry Christmas to somebody who otherwise would have no Christmas cheer. Calico toys and those cut from thin pine boxes are not hard to make, are lasting and are an unlimited pleasure to the small owners.

Give your children a full share in making Christmas. Permit them to trim the tree, put up the usual decorations and help with the baking and extra cooking. Give them a chance to enjoy the Christmas hustle, bustle, sights, smells and sounds.

Give them the stabilizing memory of kind, generous, understanding home-folks.

The happiness of unselfishness is a gift beyond price that you may give your children this Christmas.

MRS. HAVE BEEN THERE. December 7, 1935

Please, A Little Tinsel

Long years have passed and the world has changed since Christ, our Lord, was born, but time has not erased the joy that lives each Christmas morn. For He was God's great gift to man, the Son who saved the world. He preached the gospel unto all despite the scorn that was hurled. So Christmas Day we celebrate His birth in one glad song. We sing His praise and honor Him in rejoicing throng.

L.A.B. December 25, 1937

Why I Like December

I enjoy the month of December more than any other because—

I like to watch the shoppers hurry and bustle along with their bundles and to hear them exchange merry Christmas greetings.

I like to see the children's shining faces as they view the beautifully decorated windows.

I like the sweet, spicy smell of fruit cakes, mince pies, and puddings in the kitchen.

I like to hear the music of popping corn, soon to be made into colorful balls.

I like to see the gay packages piled high to be mailed to relatives and friends.

I like to hear the whispering and scampering of the children as they hide their gifts away.

I like to hear the children sing and hum the Christmas songs that they are learning at school.

I notice that the crunching of the snow beneath our feet as we hurry along sounds like music.

The cheerful blaze in the fireplace seems brighter than usual as we sit by it and read a bit after an unusually busy day.

I like to feel that although the world is at swords-point, at heart men are not bad, and that they really wish that there might be lasting peace and good will to all men.

MRS. L.G.H. December 14, 1935

Light Of Christmas

That holy night, 2000 years ago, a radiant new star appeared in the velvet curtain of our earthly sky. Steadfastly throughout the ages it has been bringing brightness and cheer to a dark, dreary world. Whenever the light from this star falls on the lives of men, it glorifies them—for it is the perfect white light, formed by the ideal blending of all pure-colored rays.

As the light for the star passes thru the prism of human living, it is separated into its primary colors, disclosing the secret of its great power.

In it is the flaming red ray of courage; the ray that makes living an art, not a mere existence; a ray needed more at present than ever.

The golden glow of love turns the drabness of duty into a shining glory—because of the yellow light of unselfishness, the simple happenings of the common day become "events."

The restful green days of faith and hope soften the glare of fear, sickness and sorrow.

'Tis the royal blue of steadfastness of purpose and loyalty that make it possible for the worker to carry on.

Not all the colors in this light are showy ones; there is need for the somber indigo of dependability and perseverance. At the outer edges is a tinge of violet—tolerance, forbearance, and patience.

All these lovely things: flaming courage, shining love, ennobling unselfishness, ever-living faith and hope, true-blue loyalty, solid reliability and gentle charity are gifts of the light— merged they form the sacred rays from the silver Star of Bethlehem.

MRS. H.S.W. December 21, 1935

It's The Last Month Of The Year

The last month of the year, and what do we see? Hustle and bustle and a Christmas tree. Not enough money, too much to do; three cranky children with a touch of the flu. Apples and candy and nuts— to date, five pounds too many of added weight. Gifts to wrap and cards to send, a letter to write to a far-away friend. Some cookies to take to a neighbor who's ill, to give her lonely heart a thrill.

The Bible is open to Luke, Chapter 2, and we leave for awhile the work still to do; to reread the story of love and light, which seems every year to grow more and more bright.

Best, Christmas Eve in the small church we love, with a manger, a baby, a bright star above. Children's faces shine in the flickering candle glow, as they tell in song and pageant of the baby born long ago. For Christmas time is busy, and full of joy and fun, but we must not forget it comes because God sent

HIS SON. December 3-10, 1968

Better Than Usual

A month ago when the Christmas decorations began to appear, I made up my mind this year we would not even make a pretense of celebrating Christmas. It will be the second year our oldest child has been in the Pacific area, and with so much sorrow and unhappiness, a celebration seemed hollow. Last year the other children wanted to go on as usual, and I made a valiant effort. We had a Christmas tree with all the decorations we had used for years. There was one particular one—an angel for the top of the tree—that the children always fought over who should be allowed to place it. When we found that, there was nothing said, it was just put back in the box. At Christmas dinner I tried to have the things he did not like. Thought that would make it easier—no one else liked them either! It was all such a flop that I decided we just wouldn't attempt it this year.

Then this letter came from overseas. I'll give it to you in part: "I hope this will get to you at least a week before Christmas, because then you'll know that I'm doing it all with you this year. Last year I was on my way over, so I didn't have a chance to write you how I would think about all you were doing, knowing that Christmas would be going on in the same bangy way. I'll be thinking about that tree decorating, and you kids better get your turn now at that angel. I'll be putting her up several years to come to make up for the times I'm missing—understand? Then when it comes to the dinner, remember to have chestnuts in that turkey dressing, lots of mashed potatoes with pools of melted butter and milk—just gobs of milk—and each of you take a big glass for me.

"Mom, if it wouldn't be too much trouble, could you ask Mrs. Jones to have dinner with you? You know Bob was always my buddy, and since he is away, she'll be alone. I hate to think of people being alone on Christmas. Could you do something for Mrs. Johnson, too? The last I heard Fred was 'missing'—golly I hate that. I know you all are going to miss me just as I am missing you, but don't worry about me a minute. Some way this last year I have grown up. Over here we all seem to have the same idea of helping the other fellow. We have the real Christmas spirit, and if you have that, you can't be lonesome at Christmas no matter where you are..."

How thankful I am that this letter came in time for me to "right-about-face." The Christmas tree stands high and brave with the angel at the very tip-top, put there laughingly by the other children. Mrs. Jones and Mrs. Johnson will be on hand for Christmas dinner. They were both here this afternoon helping with preparations. If an occasional lump has come in my throat I have swallowed it in a hurry, saying to myself, "If you have the real Christmas spirit, you can't be lonesome at Christmas no matter where you are."

Yes, we'll have Christmas at our house this year, and it will be better than usual.

E.W.S. December 16, 1944

Christmas, Not X-Mas

Oh, why leave the Christ out of Christmas,
And substitute X for His name?
There is naught else on earth or in heaven,
Can ever make Christmas the same.

Be it thoughtlessness, haste or indifference,
By the way I grieve and offend,
When I leave the Christ out of Christmas,
I am slighting my very best friend.

When I leave out the Christ in Christmas,
In vain is my holiday mirth,
For the God Christ's best gift to His children,
Is the Christ that brought Christmas to earth.

God forgive me this thoughtless omission,
I would not that He should part,
Not only the Christ of the Yuletide,
But all the year in my heart.

—Author Unknown. December 24, 1938

Spirit Of Christmas

It is Christmas time again and the peace on earth for which we hoped has still not come, but let's try at least to fill our hearts with good will toward men, which is the meaning of Christmas. Let's trim our trees as before, let's give gifts to those we love and to the needy at our gates. Sure, you're worried; many of you have known loss and heart-breaking sorrow. But the boys over there, many of them sick and sorrowful, too, want to think of that tree in the same old corner, the easy chair, the fellowship of Christmas time. They are fighting for it; it is something to come back to, the spirit and belief of Christmas.

So let's go forth with a smile, even though we have to practice a little first. And if we can't wish our neighbor and the stranger at our door "Merry Christmas," we can change it to "Happy Christmas," for happiness is deeper than just being merry; it is the joy of the sunshine, the birds' songs, the beautiful things around us, and the gay laughter of a happy child. We will have only one Christmas 1944, so let's make it bright. Give some small girl with a worn coat and shabby shoes that big doll in the window; some small boy who will have but little to rejoice with this year the bright toy his heart longs for, and watch the very spirit of Christmas come alive in their faces.

MRS. HAPPY CHRISTMAS. December 16, 1944

No Mistaking It

We are virtually drowned in seals and tinsel and mystery here at our house. Father comes home with the queerest bulges in his pockets. Wonderful smells linger in the kitchen. Mother rustles tissue paper after we are all in bed. John is making footstools from soap boxes and old stove legs. Lola is making cedar wreaths. Ellen is dipping pine cones in copper sulfate for a colorful fire. Sally, only 4, is clamoring to string more popcorn and cranberries for the tree.

Umm—do you s'pose Christmas could be coming?

ONE OF SEVEN. December 17, 1938

He Listened In Awe

I was teaching in a rural school in the short-grass country of Western Kansas. As I told the simple Christmas story, it proved to be entirely new to one of my first-grade boys! The beauty and wonder of the story seemed to make a deep impression on him.

Throughout the season he spoke of "the little baby Jesus" in a hushed tone and manner that I love to recall. When things tend to get "cluttered up," I think of this boy's response. Then Christmas again becomes something out of this world. Magic must mean that. And the memory of a little boy's face when he heard the story of the nativity for the very first time never fails to induce

CHRISTMAS MAGIC. December 20, 1955

When the Family Goes To Church

Christmas! What a joyous time! With all the hustle and time consuming things to do, my favorite time comes on Christmas Eve.

In our large family we attend different churches. Because the minister is elderly in the church that I attend, the teenagers in our family prefer to attend another church where the minister is young—just out of college. But on Christmas Eve, we all attend midnight mass at the Catholic Church. I should also add that our husband and father also attends at this time with us. He doesn't go to church; only for special programs.

There is a special feeling in the air at midnight. You wonder if the animals really can speak at this time. Usually, the ground is covered with snow and the heavens are full of stars. What a wonderful feeling to be in church, filling a pew. We do not take part in the Catholic services, but what beautiful services they are. Anyone can visit and is made welcome.

Then back home with a glow of close feeling still with you. It makes a very close family. You have time for a little rest before the family is up for their presents.

May every family feel the blessings of Christ in the coming

SEASON. December 15, 1970

The Real Meaning

I wonder sometimes if we don't forget to stress the fact that Christmas is the birthday of Christ, and perhaps depend a little too much upon the Santa Claus side when we talk about that holiday to our youngsters.

Our teacher always has a birthday party for her first and second graders. It supplies the children with a reading lesson, writing lesson, etc., and they get so much enjoyment from it. She has two little red bells that one of the class rings in honor of the child whose birthday they are celebrating.

Last year, during the Christmas season, the mothers were invited to the little Christmas tree. An eighth-grade girl told the story of Jesus to the little folks. She stressed the fact that Christmas is celebrated in honor of Jesus' birthday. After the story was finished, the teacher asked if the children had any suggestions of something else to do before the gifts were presented. A sweet little blond-haired child arose and softly said, "Shouldn't we ring the birthday bells for Jesus?"

With all sincerity, a smile playing in her bright blue eyes, she rang them. The entire class sat still and watched devotedly. The teacher, tears in her eyes, said to us, the visiting mothers, "Can you imagine a more impressive devotional hour?"

I REALLY COULD NOT. December 23, 1939

Worship Under The Stars

Every time I have a chance to stand out under a starry December sky, I can't help thinking how much of the Christmas story took place out of doors.

Joseph and Mary and their long journey to Bethlehem. The shepherds on the hills. The star in the sky. The song of the angels. The coming of the Wise Men.

Christmas is a wonderful time to worship a bit more than usual in the wonderful out of doors!

ADELE. December 25, 1948

A Gift Lies In A Manger

Christmas is a time for old and young to be happy. But this year many will say it is impossible to be happy with our sons, husbands and fathers away, over there where the true Christmas festival has been abolished. Many a gift has been sent across to help cheer the loved ones and to remind them the season has come again. But the gift idea is only a symbol of the great gift given almost 2000 years ago. We Americans still possess the freedom of worship, and as the Christmas season dawns again let us remember that in spite of war, fears and disappointments, we still have reason to be happy. Let us never take Christ out of Christmas, so that we may always find happiness at this season. And may all Americans observe the holiday season with thanksgiving.

AN AMERICAN. December 23, 1944

Loans Cap And Coat

When I was 7 years old (now 81), we were living with my grandparents in Nebraska. My father had died in Iowa the year before. That year, my grandfather had bought himself a brand-new overcoat with a black felt hat to match. One morning just before Christmas, he walked to the post office in his new outfit, but returned home in a moth-eaten and tattered coat and old cap.

Grandmother took one look at my grandpa and said, "John, what happened to your good coat and hat?" He told her he met Bert at the post office. Bert's daughter had just died in Lincoln. When Grandpa asked if Bert was going to Lincoln he said he couldn't.

So Grandpa took off his new coat and hat and gave them to Bert along with money for a ticket, telling him he had an hour to catch the train.

Bert brought the coat and hat home later in the week, saying he would pay Grandpa the money as soon as he could. Grandpa said, "Just think of it as a Christmas gift from me to you." I could see the tears on the old man's face as he thanked

GRANDPA. December 20, 1988

Family Knows The Joy Of Christmas Giving

For years Christmas was a hassle around our house. With four children and a 10-year range in ages, it seemed like all I heard from the time the Christmas catalogues arrived was, "I want" and "You can't have that, I want it."

Although they attended church regularly and knew where Christmas came from, it still didn't seem to get through to them that the spirit of giving was more important than a gift received.

One Christmas my Sunday School class decided that instead of exchanging gifts with one another we would adopt a family and fix Christmas for them. This included a complete new outfit for each member, at least one toy for each child, Christmas dinner and stocking treats, plus used clothing and staple groceries.

The family we selected had 11 children. The oldest was 16 with a child of her own. They lived at the lowest level of poverty, even though their father drove a truck for the county. It is doubtful any of them had ever had anything new. My children went to school with them and knew the situation. From the time they heard what we planned to do, they wanted to know what they could do. They decided to make each child who was young enough (that came to eight) a stuffed animal. Mine had a regular menagerie, mostly homemade, and had played with them constantly for years.

I chose fairly simple patterns and let them have at it. They worked on this for several weeks, and nobody was more thrilled when the gifts were delivered than the children who had made them.

From that time on, although they still ask for things for Christmas, their previous selfishness has never been expressed. About September they start wanting to know who our family will be this year. The simple act of one child making a stuffed animal for another seemed to teach what I hadn't been able to: the real meaning of Christmas and the true joy of giving. Two of my children are grown, and the other two are teenagers, but for 14 years this annual task has been a blessing to both my Sunday School class and my

FAMILY. December 23, 1980

Church Bells Best

With so many lovely sounds that I've enjoyed through the years, it's hard to select the best. But I believe the most beautiful sound in my later years is the clear sound of a church bell ringing on Sunday morning. It may be the bell at our own church, or it may be the one from a church on the other side of our small town. But it carries a message that we get in no other way.

When it rings out so loud and clear on Christmas morning, we are reminded of the first Christmas and its message being carried around the world. So I'll say again that the church bell has the sweetest sound

TO ME. December 7, 1971

Don't Miss The Real Meaning

I know there are people who dread Christmas because they feel alone and left out with no near relatives or friends, and I feel sorry for them. Not because they are alone but because they are missing the whole meaning of Christmas, the built-in glow of sharing with others.

No one decreed that holidays are to be shared only with kith and kin. When our family dwindled from near 40 to only my husband and myself we didn't sit back and feel lonesome. We went looking for Christmas guests. You can find them everywhere: through your church, in old-folks homes, working girls away from home, young married folk who cannot afford to go home, college students, people stranded by unexpected weather, neighbors who are also alone. We never sit down to a Christmas dinner by ourselves.

I feel compassion for those who complain about being lonely on Christmas Day, but I think they need to examine their own hearts. Are they too self-centered to think of others, to put out the effort of doing for others? It needn't be an elaborate dinner with all the trimmings. Soup and sandwiches can be a feast if they are shared, and Christmas is for

SHARING. December 4, 1973

229

Gifts Given From The Heart Have No Price Tag
It's that time of the year again. The radio gives us a countdown of days before Christmas. Although I start early, there are always last-minute gifts to even up things for the grandchildren.

When I was a kid gifts came from the heart, without a price tag. A couple of years ago, my sister and I parked the car, preparing to get in on last-minute bargains on Christmas Eve. We noticed a family of seven: a mother, dad, three boys and two girls, standing in front of a large Christmas tree and nativity scene on the court-house lawn. Unlike most, who observed with a quick glance and went on, they were thoroughly enjoying each detail.

The smallest girl, about 4 years old, kneeled by the manger scene, then planted a kiss ever so lightly on the face of baby Jesus. As my sister and I walked behind the family down the street, they stopped at each display in the stores.

Later in the evening, while looking for a pair of driving gloves, I saw the mother and children trying to decide between a packet of yellow and brown jersey gloves. They finally decided and paid for them, amid smiles and chatter.

A few minutes later, I saw the children in the basement house-wares department with their dad. The purchase this time was six white coffee mugs. Amid rounds of smiles one kid said, "Won't Mommy be surprised."

I came home that Christmas with the biggest bargain I ever got—the realization that Christmas doesn't come with a price tag, but with the love radiating from our family, and the love of knowing Christ as our
SAVIOR. December 22, 1992

Coming Of Christmas Melts A Cold Heart
Who needs Christmas? I do. I live alone on Social Security. It's an endless chore and a losing battle trying to stretch a limited income to cover the cost of living. People tend to become selfish as we grow older. All we can think of is self-preservation. Yet, with the coming of Christmas something seems to melt my cold heart. I

become more mellow and begin to think of others. I haven't money to spend on gifts, but I can still use my mind and hands. Pack rat that I am, my scrap bag is full of potential. There are so very many small gifts I can make. And the more I make, the more I want to do. Soon I have several boxes filled with potholders, bookmarks, pin cushions, small rag-and-yarn dolls and animals. For several weeks before and after Christmas, as long as my supply lasts, anyone young or old who comes to call can choose a gift if they wish. I make it understood I want nothing in return; these are my "thank yous" for kindness shown me throughout the year.

I call on shut-ins and take them a book, cookies, jam or home-baked bread. I find that all through Christmas I'm well and happy and filled with love. I call my granddaughters and tell them to bring their little ones to me while they shop. I love having them, though I'm worn out when they leave. But it's Christmas and I don't mind. I can even overcome some of the pettiness we old ladies like to indulge in at times.

This lasts for several months. Then it seems the price of meat rises, my furnace or some appliance needs repairs and then I'm back to grumbling and counting pennies again. Yes, Christmas is for children, but I believe everyone needs it, especially older people, just as much or perhaps a little bit

MORE. December 2-9, 1975

Christmas Wishes

If I could choose my own birthday I'd have it come on Christmas. I think that would be the loveliest time. Christmas children are bound to be different. The very stillness of the nights and the brightness of the stars and the good will in everybody's hearts reflects in a baby born at Christmas. And what a thrill to know that all the world was giving gifts on my birthday! I'd like to have the same birthday as the baby Jesus and I'd feel I was sharing a tiny bit of honor with Him on His beautiful day.

ANN. December 24, 1938

Stranger Has Christmas Spirit

Inside their parked car, a father, mother and their children waited impatiently for the Santa Claus parade. At last it appeared, and the parents spread a quilt on top of the car and set the children on it so they would miss none of the Christmas parade.

Nearby a shabbily dressed man holding a little girl by the hand asked hesitantly, "Would you mind if I put this little girl on top of your car?" "Not a bit," said the father, "put her up." The stranger took off his coat, wrapped the girl in it, and set her atop the car. The parade was colorful and exciting. The children screamed and clapped their hands as Santa went by. The stranger in his shirt sleeves shivered with cold and blew on his hands to warm them.

After the final float passed, the children were lifted from the car. The stranger put on his coat, said "Thank you," and led the little girl back to a frail mother who was waiting with a tiny baby in her arms. The man placed the girl's hand in the woman's, tipped his hat and walked quickly away. He was a stranger to the mother and child, too.

It's a good world that has men who will give up their warm coats and stand in the cold so a strange child may see Santa Claus. It is a wonderful world, and the spirit of Christmas is in the hearts of many strangers in our

MIDST. December 23, 1958

Mom's Still A Firm Believer In Santa Claus

My three sons confronted me the other day with the dismaying information that there really isn't a Santa Claus. That means that there is only one believer left in the family—me! I was horrified. It's really bad enough that the boys have crossed over to the enemy camp but to try to convince me, their mother, that there is really no Santa is terrible. Despite all their arguments for their case, they haven't convinced me. I'll always be a believer.

I really don't know how I could manage Christmas without the old gentleman. The rest of the year, I'm up to my neck in ordinary-but-necessary jobs, such as cleaning, cooking, taking the boys to the dentist, and the pup to the vet, not to mention the washing, ironing and mending. But suddenly, come December, I can spend whole days shopping, wrapping gifts, addressing cards, decorating the house and trimming the tree; the marvelous part of it all is that I'm still going strong by December 25. The rest of the year it's a momentous task to put together a simple dessert for dinner, but in December I spend days in the kitchen baking and decorating holiday cookies and making fancy cakes and candies. I not only supply my own household but have plenty to give to the neighbors and relatives.

At other times, I barely manage to serve three hurried meals a day, sort a few socks, do a little ironing, and zip through the house with the vacuum cleaner, hitting only the high spots.

Using a standard mother's working day of 16 hours, there just isn't enough time to get ready for Christmas, even if you start in January. Help has to come from somewhere. Being a practical person, the only explanation I can think of is that the jolly little gentleman in the red suit is doing his bit.

Take the matter of money. Most parents I know are always short of cash. That just naturally follows having a family. Eleven months of the year, our food budget is strained to the breaking point, but in December extra goodies are abundant. We even manage to give a couple of parties.

It's always a strain getting everyone outfitted for school, and managing new winter coats for everyone is a monumental task. But come Christmas, everyone's heart's desire is indulged; and not a soul is forgotten. It's really a financial impossibility, but we haven't been hauled off to debtors' prison yet.

And who can deny that the whole atmosphere changes at Christmas? When people ask, "How are you? It's no longer just a conventional phrase; they really mean it. For a short while peace and friendliness do prevail, but how can I convince my enlightened sons that Santa Claus really has a hand in it all?

I'll just keep believing in the jolly little elf. After all, he's one of the nicest spirits I know—the spirit of
LOVE. December 15, 1970

It's The Magic Of Christmas

Times change, people change, but Christmas remains the same. For all of us it is a special time to share with others some of what God has given us, in the same spirit with which He gave it; and, for this brief season, we are willing. Ill will is set aside, old hurts and slights forgiven or overlooked as we temporarily close our book of complaints and, forgetting self for a short time, look about for ways of spreading a little happiness. We glow with a feeling of brotherhood as we experience a closer communion with God and mankind.

Christmas waves a magic wand over us and we are filled to the brim with happiness; we bubble over with laughter, good cheer and good deeds. Christmas is a fact and a faith, a renewal of hope to carry us through the coming year; but even if it were only a brief season of good will, a short respite in our forgetfulness of others, a time when families are reunited, a moment of awe as we review the ancient miracle of birth; then it would be worth it. These things about Christmas do not

CHANGE. December 7, 1971

Just What Are We Celebrating?

My wish is that this Christmas, we who call ourselves Christians would celebrate in honor of Christ, rather than celebrating ourselves again.

It is convenient for us wishing to celebrate with gifts, festivities, yes, and even with drink to say that Christmas comes at such a busy time of year. It's another excuse to celebrate ourselves. It's also convenient for the merchants who depend on Christmas sales to make the difference between operating at a loss or a profit for the year. We've made it a celebration of we know not what nor whom, except ourselves. Maybe we're caught up in giving gifts—but most of them are to our loved ones. But how many really believe that showing love in the true meaning would also include those who may not be relatives or friends?

Two questions might embarrass us: Do I really know the true Christmas message? Do I know how to tell the message of Christ

and His message of love to another person? If we really understood the message of Christmas and weren't too embarrassed to
tell it, maybe we would invite someone less fortunate into our
home to share a Christmas meal. Or we might share a pair of
outgrown children's shoes with the barefoot child next door.

It's incriminating that a nation calling itself "Christian" is so
self-centered at the most joyous time of year. It's incriminating that in
memory of Christ—who came to Earth to demonstrate God's
love—we "Christians" see the market flooded with military toys; our
Christian nation spends $4 million to keep land out of production
while tens of thousands are starving daily; this nation involves itself
in defense spending exceeding $100 billion a year.

Is God really pleased with our Christmas carols being sung in
fabulous churches with no invitations for outsiders to come share
the joy of
> CHRISTMAS? December 3-10, 1968

In Celebration Of A Birthday

What do I like best about Christmas? I like a tree with ornaments and tinsel, under whose sheltering branches are piled my
gifts for family and friends. I like the lights that twinkle from
homes and buildings—blue and yellow, red and green. Even the
traffic lights seem to be celebrating the season.

I like the bells that ring from church steeples, calling us to worship. And the bells that ring beside the familiar kettles on street
corners, reminding us to give generously to those less fortunate.

I like the uplift of my heart whenever the manger story is told
or "Silent Night" is sung. I like the faith of Christmas—the reality
of a living God and His loving Son. For Christmas faith is truth
and goodness; it is the very spirit of hope and joy, of kindness and
blessings.

But above all, I like Christmas because it is the birthday of He
who came to lead us in the paths of understanding, love and
peace; to show us the way of life, abundant and
> ETERNAL. November 30, 1971

Child Led The Way

The first Christmas that I was a widow I felt I could never have the Christmas spirit again. I didn't want a tree or any part of Christmas. I only wanted the day over and forgotten.

Before I was widowed, Christmas was looked forward to with great joy. We were a close family; our children, their families and any lonely person was always welcome in our home. Now all was different.

Then, a few days before Christmas, my 5-year-old grandson was spending the day with me. "When are you going to get your Christmas tree, Grandma?" he asked. "May I help decorate it if I'm real careful?" He did not doubt that I would have a tree and I could not disappoint him.

So I regained the Christmas spirit in the best way of all, through a little

CHILD. December 22, 1959

In The True Spirit

Popcorn and cranberry strings are traditional at Christmas, but for me they are special.

Six years ago this Christmas we had been married one year, and our baby was a month old. We were 500 miles from our families, and we had made few friends in our new town. My husband was in college then, and money was something we often dreamed of, but never had. Our carefully saved reserve had been spent when the baby was born, and as December 25 drew near, the prospect was for a dreary holiday.

Nevertheless, I strung a cranberry chain and a longer popcorn chain (popcorn goes a long way) and hung them over the windows, trying to capture some of the festive Christmas spirit. They looked a little forlorn, but it was the best I could do.

Christmas morning I lay in bed with my eyes closed, thinking of our loneliness in a strange place. I could hear my husband moving around in the other room and thought he must be carrying out the ashes and poking the fire so the house would get warmed up.

In a little while, he came in and whispered, "Merry Christmas! Come on, get up!"

When I stepped into the living room, there in splendor stood my husband's gift to me. It was a folding clothes rack, artfully draped with loops of popcorn and cranberry strings. Underneath were the boxes from our families ready to be opened.

How he knew that I had been yearning for a rack so I wouldn't have to hang out diapers in the freezing cold, or how he managed to get the few extra dollars to buy it, I don't know. But I do know that I never celebrate Christmas without some popcorn and cranberry strings to remind me of that shining Christmas when I learned that the smallest gift is made great
BY LOVE. December 8, 1953

A Child's Christmas

Never a Christmas season draws near that I do not relive the days of my childhood. We were poor—so didn't spend a great deal of money for gifts—but our Christmas spirit was not lacking.

I was greatly impressed that the Christ Child was born in a manger. It seemed such a peaceful place to me. I would sit in the manger on sweet-smelling hay while my parents milked by lantern light. On Christmas Eve I would pretend that Mary and the Christ Child were in our barn. It was a lovely game and as we walked to the house when chores were finished, I was a very happy little girl.

Time has changed many customs, but the beautiful simplicity of Christmas in the country cannot be changed. I am no longer a little girl, but a grandmother with a sprinkling of silver in my hair. Yet today, I like to walk into the barn on Christmas Eve; in the quiet peacefulness of cattle feeding it is not difficult to imagine the scene of so long ago.

I hope I will be able to teach my grandchildren of the beauty and peace surrounding our Savior's birth.
PEACEFUL. December 25, 1956

Christmas Recipe

Take the crisp cold of a December night, add two generous parts of snow, stir in air so clear it tinkles. Into a generous heart, mix the wonder of a little girl, the sparkle of a young boy's glance, the love of parents, and set gently before the chimney side. Add the lightest touch of reindeer's hooves, a sprig of holly, a scent of fir. Set the mixture to rise in the warmth of a dream of good will to men. It will be almost ready to serve when it bubbles with warmth and good feeling. Bedeck with the light of a star set in the East, garnish with shining balls of gold, silver and red. Serve to the tune of an ancient carol in the middle of the family table. This recipe is sufficient for all the men and women you will ever meet.

ANONYMOUS. December 25, 1956

Hints For Mrs. Santa

Of course it is not Christmas time yet, but you will be surprised how soon it will be here.

What I have in mind takes a little time, a little understanding and very little work. But it will gladden the hearts of some folks who might be able to use a little more gladness.

Give a little gift to the old lady down the street or to the poor-but-busy mother across the street. Give to some who are not on your regular Christmas list.

Time will be needed to see what flower the old lady might like. Now is the time to paint a coffee can a pretty shade of green and to fill it with rich soil and get your flower cutting started. By Christmas it will be growing nicely and ready to give.

A little understanding of the busy mother and the desires of her children might lead you to gather a bag of different kinds of nuts to add glamour to their Christmas candy and cookies. Now is the time to gather nuts.

Maybe an invalid, or anyone who likes to read, would like some special magazine. Collect a stack and have them ready.

It is so much easier to plan these gifts ahead of time and get them delivered just before your own Christmas rush hour. You can find someone in their families who will act as Santa Claus for you. These are small gifts, but you can dress them up and they will carry your Christmas message. The giving of these gifts will bring you and others more happiness than the alligator dressing case you give to rich Aunt Clara.

TRY IT. November 6, 1948

"Sub For Santa" Club

For the last several years our daily paper has sponsored a "Sub for Santa" club. They obtain a list of needy people, the number in each family, conditions in the home, size of the house, ages, etc. Then the correspondent calls and writes a true-to-life story about each family.

Their names are withheld from the printed story but are given out to anyone who wishes to "sub" for Santa and adopt that family or a similar one for Christmas. Everyone in the county is asked to turn in the names of any worthy family for investigation. Anyone who desires to adopt a family or a lonely person for Christmas contacts the paper and is given the opportunity to visit their home.

Sometimes the adopted person or family is taken into their home. Sometimes the folks fix gifts, treats and a dinner and go to the home of their adopted family. Often the gifts, treats and dinner are just delivered at the home of the adopted family. As the families are adopted a record is kept of who adopted whom and the names are checked off.

The day before Christmas six different clubs and lodges send out invitations to the remaining families to attend the mass dinner held in one of the lodge halls. All four theaters in the town give out free tickets to every child listed. The tickets are good any time during the day or evening. The tickets are given to the children but the parents are welcome to accompany them.

The first week in December the stories are started—five or six each day—and everyone is given an opportunity to share either with a lonely person, a whole family or at the mass dinner.

G. December 13, 1941

Hyacinths For The Soul

One Christmas I needed so many things. In fact, about every-thing—good, sensible shoes, warm underwear—even a sack of flour would have come in handy. But the gift that came from my wealthy aunt was a lovely nightgown—a silky, wispy thing with lace and ribbon and a rosebud.

"What a fool!" said this one to that one. "To give that useless fluff when practical things are so sorely needed."

But I gloried in my gift. It warmed my soul as completely and far more satisfactorily than long underwear could have warmed my limbs. A heart filled with the joy of my bit of finery was as hunger-quenching as a stomach filled with biscuits. And it shed discouragement and fear of the future as shoes would have shed damp and mud.

My aunt isn't living now, but my thanks to her is still in my heart. And I've tried, since I'm once more in the Christmas-giving class myself, to profit by her example. I give to the heart and the mind and the soul as well as to the body.

I BELIEVE I'M RIGHT. December 25, 1937

I Didn't Spend A Cent

The best Christmas I ever spent was without a cent of money. Illness accompanied by huge bills left our finances too depleted to buy gifts. So I set about making good-deed offerings instead.

First, I went to a neighbor who had five small children and whose husband was a day laborer. She could not possibly get out to do the Christmas shopping for her wee tots except to take them along. I had seen her so often returning from town on market days with her little brood, utterly exhausted. It would certainly be a task now with the rush on. I offered my services, which were accepted with the utmost gratitude. I had a rollicking time with those youngsters, but best of all was that young mother's joy when she returned to find I had her supper ready and on the table.

Next, I went to a widower friend who was struggling with the housekeeping and care of two daughters, aged 10 and 12. I helped those children clean and decorate their house for Christmas. Later I went back and helped them prepare their Christmas dinner. I was more than repaid when that young father seated himself at the table and with a relieved sigh said, "Children, it seems more like home than it has since Mother died."

A few days before Christmas I told several young neighbor girls that if they would bring their waving fluid to my house I would finger wave their hair for free. Many of them could not possibly afford a wave at a shop. Although only an amateur, the waves were pretty.

Each day presented a new opportunity. Oh! there was so much to be done, and I became so enthusiastic I forgot about having no Christmas money. Altogether, I gave 40 people happiness that lasts, for a good deed is remembered long after one has forgotten who gave the gift bought with the most money.

OKLAHOMA. December 24, 1932

The Other Wise Man

One of the most beautiful ways of keeping Christmas is for family and friends to gather on Christmas Eve for the reading of a Christmas story, and I know of no selection that better portrays the true spirit of Christmas and Christianity than *The Other Wise Man* by Henry Van Dyke. I once heard a minister review this little book for his Christmas sermon.

This beautiful modern allegory assumes that there was a fourth wise man who was to meet the others and follow with them where the star led. However, he stopped to give aid to an unfortunate wayfarer, and when he reached the appointed place, the others had gone on. He hurried on, but when he reached Bethlehem, the holy family had departed into Egypt. He started after them to present his gift, a jewel beyond price, to the Christ Child, but he could never ignore a cry of distress, and always arrived at a place only to learn the one he sought had just left.

This went on all through life, and as the Savior climbed the hill to Calvary, our belated wise man, now old and feeble, was hastening to give his gift and offer his homage when all other followers of the Master had forsaken Him. But now he realized that Jesus would have no more use for a jewel, so he stopped to sell it to give aid to one more sufferer—I believe in this case it was to buy a tortured child out of slavery—and hurried on, sad and empty-handed, to kneel and worship at the cross. When darkness fell and the earthquake came, he had not yet arrived. He realized he was too late.

As he lay grieving in the darkness, a radiance appeared before him, and in the midst of it appeared the one he had followed so faithfully, if belatedly, commending him for his life of service, reminding him that "Inasmuch as ye have done it unto the least of these, my brethren, ye have done it unto Me."

FOLLOWER. December 19, 1942

"Too Busy, Too Tired, Too Weak"

My Christmas wish, if I could have just one that would come true, would be for my husband to join me at church on Christmas morning. I think this would be the greatest gift he could give me this Christmas Day. My great joy would be overflowing with love for him, our two little girls, and Christian love for everyone.

Today we Americans are falling away from the true meaning of Christmas, not just on Christmas Day, but the whole year long. We fail to carry our love and the joys of brotherhood to every people. We fail to get involved, all too snug in our own little worlds. So it is we are all too busy, too tired, too weak, to face up to our obligations to one another.

The spiritual commitment we have to one another can be renewed at Christmas by all of us. Our values can all be sorted out, so that when we start the new year it may be one of hope, of love, and of faith in one another. We need to understand each other as Christ has shown us.

So I say that is why my wish is for our family to be together at mass and holy communion on Christmas. Material gifts will all too soon fade away, but the joys of Christmas can last a lifetime and an

ETERNITY. December 17-24, 1968

The Perfect Place

As we approach the birthday of the Christ Child, we often pause to think of His birthplace—a manger. Songs have been written and poets have spoken about His humble bed.

Did you ever walk into a barn or stable on a cold winter evening? Did you ever watch cattle feeding by lantern light? Truly, the contentment and peace that prevails is amazing. The Son of God could not have been born in a more peaceful spot. There were no discordant sounds in the stable on the eve of Christ's birth.

If Mary and Joseph had been able to find a room in the inn, crowded with people, I'm sure the birth of the precious babe would not have been so peaceful and

BEAUTIFUL. December 8, 1953

Sharing Christmas In Nigeria

It was just 40 years ago when we experienced our first Christmas in Africa. It seemed then as if we'd come to the "end of the world." Among the 9,000 people who lived within a two-mile radius of our home, there wasn't one who'd ever celebrated Christmas. There were no shopping centers, no gaily decorated trees, no brightly colored lights, no green wreaths, no church bells, no snow... nothing that spoke of Christmas. If this was to be our home, we thought, what meaning and what feeling for Christmas did we possess that we wanted to share with others?

Christmas began that year in that secluded area in Nigeria. There were 14 young men who had heard about the Christ Child and were interested in the Good News. How could we make the story of God's gift real to them?

On Christmas Eve, with the bright stars overhead, they gathered and sat in a circle around a small campfire. They feasted on roast mutton and then memorized songs that had been translated into their language. They heard the story of the Wise Men and the shepherds. The next morning, at daybreak, they gathered again and went in a group through the two nearby villages singing, stopping now and again to tell why they were

243

happy and singing. Christ made the difference, and Christmas in Nigeria began with Him.

Now at daybreak on every Christmas Day, hundreds of people gather to walk through many of the villages and towns proclaiming His love. This is still the only reason for them to celebrate Christmas. You see, I am a

MISSIONARY. December 15, 1970

Christmas Bible

Several years ago my small daughter and I gave my husband a Bible. He was not a Christian at that time, but he was a good moral person and a wonderful daddy. At first he seemed a little embarrassed at receiving a Bible. I was afraid he didn't appreciate it and was perhaps a little disappointed.

However, he read it through. Then he began asking questions about different passages and stories that he encountered. I could not answer all of them, but sent him to the pastor with part of them.

His interest in Christianity grew steadily. Our daughter was a happy little girl when her daddy became a Christian and went to Sunday School and church with us.

By this time there was another daughter, and it was really a blessing that she could not remember when Daddy wasn't in church. In fact, the first Sunday School superintendent she can remember was her daddy.

Last February our daddy lost his life suddenly in a storm. I know that we could not have gone through that tragic experience without the help and comfort of a higher power and without the knowledge that he, too, was surrendered to that power.

The older daughter, who is 17, now has her daddy's Bible, and the younger one, 8, has his wristwatch. The older girl and I are giving the little one the nicest Bible we can afford for Christmas this year—our first Christmas without Daddy. We are giving it with the prayer that it will provide as big a blessing to her through the years as the one we gave

HER DADDY. December 14, 1954

244

The Living Symbols Of Christmas

Christmas to me is the most wonderful experience of all, and I try to make it last all year. It is a time of rebirth, renewal, a fresh start; a time to set our minds on spiritual things and all the unseen things that are kept alive by those that are seen.

TREES—green emblem of the life that clothed God in flesh to show men someone beyond their own understanding.

LIGHTS—symbol of the heavens ablaze in glory that the shepherds saw the night Christ was born.

BELLS—echo the angels' voices, telling the matchless message of Christ's love.

WREATHS—symbol of God's unending love for us.

GREETING CARDS—spreading the good news of the Savior's birth and multiplying love for others.

GIFTS—symbol of God's unspeakable love; expression of love and service to God and others.

FAMILY GATHERINGS—Jesus was born into a family.

Even BABIES' SMILES at Christmas time remind us that Christ was human as well as divine.

All these are glad tidings of the newborn King! And they keep alive the unseen spiritual things like faith, hope, peace, joy, love, gentleness, long suffering, meekness, temperance and goodness that make life real and

WONDERFUL. December 15, 1970

More Of The Real Spirit

I believe that on Christmas we should give at least one gift that costs more than money. Forgive some old grudge that has been growing through the years. Renew some long-broken friendship. Gifts like these require real sacrifice, but they mean something more than a tissue-wrapped trinket. It's more what the real Christmas spirit was meant to be.

ADDIE MAE. December 18, 1937

Just Suppose

Christmas doesn't mean tinsel-covered trees, fruit cakes, turkey, family gatherings, crowded stores and people hurrying with Christmas packages for gift exchanges. Busy with all these, people for years have taken Christmas pretty much for granted.

Pause and think what this old world would be like without Christmas and the things for which it stands. Suppose the three Wise Men had courted the favor of Caesar and a Roman legion had clanked across the plains of Bethlehem and taken the infant Christ? But true to the fulfillment of prophecy, under the twinkling stars in the hush of an Asiatic night, the event transpired from which all progress is dated.

To me, Christmas means keeping Christ in Christmas. With love and thought for others and a full, deep appreciation of the significance of the event, we commemorate His

BIRTHDAY. December 18-25, 1962

Go, Search For Your Christmas

I feel Christmas belongs to everyone. Anyone can find it because it is in the heart. This Christmas many are without homes. Even so, the loneliest, saddest, meanest and bitterest of us has only to open his heart and the Christmas spirit will enter.

Christmas is believing the star really did shine in that midnight sky, that the shepherds were afraid, and that the angel did come to say, "Fear not." We must believe in the beautiful and the good; that they will live long after the grimness, the loneliness, and the worries have fled.

Christmas has survived thru other centuries as weary as ours. How? Because we continue to hope. We believe happy things endure. We treasure laughter, faith, and courage much above gold.

Go in search of Christmas. Maybe you'll find it in a group singing Christmas carols, a smile on the face of a stranger, in a church, or in the glowing Christmas lights on a community tree. Go

FIND IT. December 15-29, 1970

Receive Cheerfully

In this season of giving, let us remember that there must necessarily be an equal amount of receiving. A cheerful giver, to my mind, is no more to be praised than a cheerful receiver—and we are all receivers.

Surely the cardinal rule of receiving is never to forget to acknowledge a gift, be it large or small, from someone near and dear like Aunt Minnie or from a more impersonal source—a school or lodge or other organization.

Even the little ones can write simple and brief notes to those who give to them, even though the message be limited to those two gracious words, "Thank You." It is often quoted that the Lord loveth a cheerful giver. I am sure that he also loveth a cheerful receiver and one who does not forget to express his gratefulness!

KATE. December 28, 1946

Richest Are Poorest

I am thinking of a little girl of five years who is just beginning school. She is a beautiful little creature with immaculate clothes and an intelligent mind. She is, to put it mildly, her parents' showpiece. She sings, plays the piano, is trained in speaking, etc.

This Christmas she will receive many beautiful gifts. Costly, elaborate and ornate like herself. She will give the teacher an expensive gift. Maybe she won't be any too happy herself, for she will be alone in the big house with no one to share her trinkets except, perhaps, the wonderful talking, walking doll that after all has no human heart.

How much better if the child might have part of the money to do things for her playmates. If she might be allowed to fix up, and give away some of her myriad dolls and dishes. She might learn that giving to those who need is a joy, and that there is something to Christmas besides tinsel and the jingle of many coins.

JINGLE BELLS. December 22, 1934